BRITISH MUSEUM
LONDON

Newsweek/GREAT MUSEUMS OF THE WORLD

NEW YORK, N.Y.

GREAT MUSEUMS
OF THE WORLD

Editorial Director—Carlo Ludovico Ragghianti
Assistant—Giuliana Nannicini
Translation and Editing—Editors of ARTNEWS

BRITISH MUSEUM
LONDON

Texts by:
Antonino Caleca
Decio Gioseffi
Gian Lorenzo Mellini
Licia Ragghianti Collobi

Design:
Fiorenzo Giorgi

Published by
NEWSWEEK, INC.
& ARNOLDO MONDADORI EDITORE

Library of Congress Catalog Card No. 68-20025

THE BRITISH MUSEUM: FOREWORD

SIR FRANK FRANCIS
Director and Principal Librarian

Museums, particularly the world's great museums, are the repositories of the remains of past civilizations. They provide the place where these civilizations can be studied and where their cultural achievements can be understood and appreciated. The prime purpose of a great museum is to collect materials for the comprehensive and intensive study of the past, and as such they are the resort of scholars. But they afford also to the ordinary man and woman opportunities for appreciating the qualities and the achievements of the human beings who were part and parcel of these great civilizations. They enable us all to see and to draw inspiration from the grace and virility of sculptures of the Greeks, the impassive granite figures of Egypt, the strength of Rome, the sensitiveness of Assyrian animal carvings, the patience and superb craftsmanship of the so-called Dark Ages and the religious intensity of medieval times.

The British Museum, the first "public" as distinct from "private" museum in the world, has been engaged in these tasks for over 200 years. Founded on the basis of the comprehensive collections of Sir Hans Sloane, and enriched over the years by the acquisition of other great collections and by specially commissioned excavations, it is one of the richest museums in the world. Its collections of British and medieval, Greek and Roman, Egyptian, Western Asiatic and Far Eastern antiquities, of ethnographical specimens, of coins and medals, of prints and drawings, manuscripts and printed books provide outstanding riches for the scholar and countless treasures for the interested visitor.

The museum curator has a fourfold responsibility. He must collect; he must preserve; he must ensure that the treasures in his care are made available in the most appropriate and fruitful way for students; and he must see that the treasures in his care are made known as widely as possible. Exhibitions and gallery displays are of course the most appropriate means of doing this; publication is another. Modern photographic techniques and procedures of reproduction are so advanced that it is possible nowadays by means of convincing and beautiful illustrations to make known to many people in all parts of the world who are never likely to see them with their own eyes, the outstanding objects of the world's great collections.

This is the reason why I am highly gratified at this opportunity of bringing some knowledge of the treasures of the British Museum to the people of America. The quality of the illustrations in the volumes of this magnificent series is very high indeed, and I know of no better means of familiarizing the public with these important objects of antiquity and of demonstrating the pervasiveness of those human qualities of ingenuity, craftsmanship and love of beauty which are common to all the peoples of the world.

PREFACE

FREDERICK S. LEIGH–BROWNE

The British Museum is unique among national museums in having been founded simultaneously as a great library and as an all-embracing museum. The British Museum is, moreover, second only to the Ashmolean Museum in Oxford as the earliest public museum of modern type to be established. Both institutions stem from that era of the late seventeenth and eighteenth centuries when the potentiality of the Museum for mankind as a means of general education as well as a center for learned research was just beginning to be realized by those in authority.

The Greek-derived word "Museum" was originally applied to a religious brotherhood for the worship of the Muses. The brethren would establish a sort of college for the furtherance of their studies: education began to be associated with the concept of "museum." But it was not until the Alexandria museum was set up by Ptolemy I about 300 B.C. that a collection of material objects came to be regarded as part of the equipment of such a research institution. It is noteworthy that Ptolemy associated his museum with a great library. In maintaining such association, the British Museum can claim to be continuing the Alexandrian tradition.

But whereas the Egyptian — or, rather, Hellenistic — museum, in common with many important museums of today, owed its inception to the beneficence of a monarch, the British Museum derives its character and constitution from the individual genius of an English savant — of Irish birth, it is true — of the eighteenth century, namely Sir Hans Sloane. The era of his lifetime came on the heels of the great European awakening of the Renaissance, when the pursuit of knowledge and truth had extended even to distant parts of the earth in the great voyages of discovery. Savants and the wealthy alike now took the opportunity of amassing collections of exotic rarities in their "academies" and "cabinets." But such collections were only rarely accessible to the general public, and most of them, unscientifically assembled as they were, would in any case have been of little value for the purpose of general education.

Sir Hans Sloane (1660–1753), famous physician and President of the Royal Society from 1727 to 1740, collected what he himself in his will enumerated *inter alia* as "books, drawings, manuscripts, prints, medals and coins ancient and modern, antiquities, seals . . . precious stones . . . mathematical instruments . . . and pictures." He expressed the wish that his collection should be offered to the Crown — that is, to the nation — for twenty thousand pounds sterling, one-fourth of its cost to himself, to be kept "for the use and improvement of the arts and sciences, and benefit of mankind."

Parliament seized the opportunity thus offered, set up a body of Trustees from among high dignitaries of church and state, and authorized them to organize a lottery — the exchequer being impoverished — to purchase the Sloane collection as well as the Harleian manuscripts that were then also available and to provide a "general repository" for these two libraries as well as for the Cottonian library, already acquired for the nation in 1700. A repository or "home" for the collections was found in Montagu House, a red-brick town residence of the late seventeenth century that stood on the site of the present Museum.

The act of Parliament declared that the collections "and any additions to them" should remain in the repository to be preserved "for public use, to all posterity," and that free access to them should be granted "to all studious and curious persons." Thus there was enunciated the basic principle of the modern museum: it is to be available for public education (to the "studious") and for public recreation (to the "curious"). But the British Museum still suffered from one great disadvantage of the *"cabinets de curiosités"* that had preceded it: it was essentially still, despite public ownership, a private collection in a private dwelling.

Sir Hans Sloane's collection, encyclopedic in character with its 69,352 items apart from books and manuscripts, was disposed on the two upper floors of the house in three departments: manuscripts, medals and coins; natural and artificial products; printed books, maps, globes, drawings, etc. There were study and store rooms on the ground floor. It was not until 1807 that the first reorganization occurred, when the "natural history" department was divided into two sections, for "natural history and modern curiosities" and "antiquities and coins." This was the first of many such rearrangements, but well into the nineteenth century the British Museum maintained the characteristic of a mélange of assorted items from an infinity of sources, as can be observed in some of the watercolors of George Scharf.

Meanwhile, the Museum, like a magnet, attracted to itself other collections, and the Trustees were constrained to seek parliamentary approval for extensions to the buildings. Eventually, the transfer of the library of King George III in 1823 to a Museum already overcrowded provided the stimulus for the erection of a new building in classical Greek style on the same site. This edifice designed by Mr. (later Sir) Robert Smirke, and built in stages between 1823 and 1852, forms the main part of the present Museum buildings.

Thus the British Museum entered on a new phase of its existence in a building which, however inadequate by today's standards, was at least specifically designed as a museum. Here was a framework within which could be worked out the transformation of the physician's collection of books and "rarities" into an institution organized to serve the needs both of popular education and of scientific research.

It would be foolish to claim that the British Museum is the ideal of a museum, but at least it has the capacity of development that could bring it as close to perfection as any earthly museum is ever likely to attain. An opportunity for a more orderly arrangement of the collections and for the provision of better facilities for study came in the period between 1878 and 1886 when the Museum's oil paintings were transferred to the national picture galleries and the natural history collections to a new Natural History Museum in Kensington near Hyde Park.

Although admission to the Museum was dependent in the eighteenth century on the observation of certain formalities, it should be remarked that, in contrast to the practice in some other countries, there never has been any fee payable by members of the public for entry, or for the use of the services of the various departments. It is only to be lamented that it is no longer practicable to offer the public the advantages enjoyed by one of the earliest users of the Museum. Since he had "occasion to make drawings of some cinnamon and cassia," the Trustees decided that the collections of dried plants containing "the said specimens be carried to him into the Reading-Room." Nonetheless, there are departmental students' rooms where duly accredited researchers can enjoy facilities similar to those available in the general Reading Room in 1759. This means that the collections are still in very close juxaposition to the library so that research in archeology, art or ethnography can be conducted under unusually favorable conditions. It is of great significance that the chief officer of the Museum has from the outset born the title of "Principal Librarian" (the additional title of "Director" being added in 1898).

In this museum-library relationship, ideas set out in the Act of Parliament establishing the Museum in 1753 find their practical expression through the physical arrangements inside the building. The preamble of the 1753 Act declared: "All arts and sciences have a connection with each other, and discoveries in natural philosophy and other branches of speculative knowledge, for the advancement and improvement whereof the said Museum or collection was intended, do — or may in many instances — give help and success to the most useful experiments and undertakings."

Sir Hans Sloane began collecting in his youth, and when, having qualified in medicine, he went to Jamaica as physician to the Governor of the colony, the Duke of Albemarle, he assembled specimens of West Indian plant and animal life. On his return to London, he published a scientific work, *The Natural History of Jamaica*. It is in direct accord with Sir Hans Sloane's procedure in this regard that the British Museum as an institution has sponsored a notable series of archeological and other investigations in various parts of the world, a practice which is now, of course, generally recognized as part of the normal activities of a great museum. The nineteenth-century excavations of the sites of Assyrian cities and of such classical Greek sites as Ephesus have been matched in importance in the twentieth century by the work of Sir Leonard Woolley at Ur in Mesopotamia. Less widely known, but of vital significance in the fields of archeology and ethnography, are the later British Museum expeditions to British Honduras and New Guinea.

The publication of the scientific findings resulting from such expeditions is as essential a part of the work of the Museum as the methodical cataloguing and annotation of the collections received from other sources, public and private. And it is a symptom of the vigor of the two-century-old British Museum that one of its departments, little known indeed to the public at large, comprises a laboratory with a range of scientific equipment available for the investigation and preservation of objects, not only in the Museum's own collections, but also in other collections in Britain and abroad.

No examination of the British Museum can fail to reveal the extent to which its collections have been, and are continually being, enriched through the zeal of private individuals, often themselves experts in a comparatively limited field in which they may even have achieved a reasonably comprehensive coverage in their material. But the ideal that inevitably lies behind all the Museum's activities — that of a survey of all cultural activity at all stages of human history — is continually urging the Museum to search diligently and with discrimination so that gaps can be filled in the record that it offers. For this purpose, funds are made available to the Museum by the British Parliament. There is, however, always scope for further financial support, and this is provided by many generous friends of the nation's museums and galleries through the National Art Collections Fund, which has facilitated the acquisition of many important items — for example, the Portland Vase.

The ultimate beneficiary from the Museum's activities is, of course, the community as a whole — and it is a community that transcends all national frontiers. But to come nearer home, tribute must be paid to those who have been conscious of the Museum's continual need for expansion in space. One such, literally a *neighbor* of the Museum, William White, made in the mid-nineteenth century a bequest that permitted the erection of a new wing (the "White Wing") at the southeast corner of the building. Fresh space was thus found for the library departments. Further improvements were envisaged in the bequest of a member of a banking family, Vincent Stuckey Lean, whose munificence, combined with funds from the government, made possible the erection between 1907 and 1914 of the King Edward VII Building, whose galleries now afford such an elegant setting for many of the Museum's treasures.

Fresh impetus to the work of the Museum was provided in 1963 when a new Act of Parliament reconstituted the governing body, provided for the final severance of the administration of the Natural History Museum from the institution that gave it birth in 1880, and empowered the Trustees to use much wider discretion than they could before in making loans from the collections on a temporary basis. At the same time, plans have been drawn up for a new library building adjacent to the present Museum. Once again, the expected changes will provide much needed space: but it is to be noted that in physical proximity the library and museum will continue to exist in the happy matrimonial state that they have enjoyed for over two centuries.

AFRICA
OCEANIA
AMERICA

IFE ART. *Oni (King) of Ife.*

It is only since the end of the last century that we know of an important artistic center of bronzes and terra cottas at Ife (in the Yoruba territory, Nigeria). According to tradition, the human figures and heads are portraits of kings. The chronology of this production has been much discussed, since it is characterized by a very high technical level and is completely different from any other African art. According to the most recent theories this sculpture is to be dated between the twelfth and fourteenth centuries. One suggestion, recently reinforced by the finding of terra cottas dating from before the birth of Christ in North Nigeria, is that a source for Ife art may be found in ancient Egypt; the style of the figures, with their compact masses, fits in with this theory. Other archeologists believe that Ife art is an independent, native phenomenon, having no connection with European (as was supposed by some) or Oriental precedents. The example in the British Museum is one of the masterpieces of this group of sculptures. It is comparable only to Egyptian works such as the heads of the IV dynasty, to late Roman heads of the fifth century or to Italian Renaissance busts by Laurana. The subtle curving pattern of the tattooing models the surface of the face, restraining the individual vitality, the lifelike quality of the statue, within a perfectly controlled sculptural mass.

BENIN ART. *Head of a Queen Mother.*   *p. 20*

Like the bronze from Ife, this statue was executed by means of the difficult "lost wax" process. It is the most beautiful of numerous examples of wood, ivory and bronze sculpture made in the Kingdom of Benin (Southern Nigeria) during the fifteenth and sixteenth centuries. Possible connections with Ife sculpture have not yet been well defined. Many Benin bronzes are descriptive and narrative in character and often exuberant in ornamentation. This rigorously formal portrait of a woman is compact, absorbed in its inwardness. It derives perhaps from the Ife style its sculptural use of pure volumes; here we easily recognize the cylinder, the oval and the cone. It goes beyond any temporary distracting realism in the balanced composition of the features. Details of hair-style, make-up and jewelry contribute to this untroubled image with its controlled inner harmony: the head-dress, eyebrows indicated by vertical strokes, hair interlaced in a basket-weave pattern, side bangs in front of crescent-shaped ears and high necklace of rings encircling the smooth neck.

IFE ART
Oni (king) of Ife
Between the 12th and 14th century.
Bronze, the crown was once red;
height 14 1/2" (life size).
Western Nigeria.

BENIN ART. *Flute Player.*

Another extraordinary example of the courtly art of Benin is this bronze cast in the "lost wax" process, then decorated with exquisitely engraved surface patterns. Representing a musician of the royal household, it was executed by a special workshop which carried out commissions for the court according to a set style. Yet we can recognize a number of individual Benin masters and a wide variety of interpretations. This production dates between the period before 1485 and the penetration of the Portuguese into Nigeria in the sixteenth century; it became known only at the time of the British conquest in 1897. The flute player is a masterpiece from Benin: standing on firm, short, pillar-like legs, the vertical, tubular figure is framed on the right within a wide arch; the arms are organized into various open triangles. The sophistication of the style also appears in the volumes of the forms themselves, the surfaces of which are modeled by the incised decoration: the rounded, cone-shaped helmet, the almond-shaped eyes and nostrils, the head inserted into the clear-cut ring of the necklace as though this were the opening of the cylindrical body, and, finally, the triangular panels of the tightly-wrapped skirt. This carefully worked out, highly structural, formal pattern gives the statue an extraordinary "classical" dignity.

BENIN ART
Head of a Queen Mother
15th–16th century.
Bronze; height 15 3/4".

BENIN ART
Flute Player
15th–16th century.
Engraved bronze;
height 24 3/8".

BAMBARA ART
Double Antelope
19th century.
Wood.

ART OF THE SOUTHERN CONGO. *King Shamba Bolongongo.*
Shamba Bolongongo was the 93rd king of the Bakuba, whose kingdom, situated between the Sankuru and Kasai rivers, lasted until the nineteenth century. He reigned from about 1600 to 1620 and was a great economic and cultural reformer, as shown here by the *mankara* in front of him, a board for an educational game. The honorary statues of the 108th and of the 190th kings, in contrast, have warlike attributes. The king was the head of a feudal system. Here he wears a crown and sits, cross-legged, on a throne. The forms are very stylized, presented as a mass in a carefully worked out symmetrical relationship with each other and the whole. Even the austere relief decoration of crown, body and base is strongly geometric, creating a rhythm which combines with the four-sided mass of the figure to create a consistent stability.

ART OF THE SOUTHERN CONGO
King Shamba Bolongongo
17th century.
Wood, partially painted;
height 21 3/4".

BAMBARA ART. *Double Antelope.*
This was an emblem used by the Bambara — an agricultural people who lived west of the great bend of the Niger River — for planting and harvest dances. It is the symbol of Chi Wara, hero and demigod, first mythical
22 cereal-grower. There are several variants of this motif. We have here a

BALSOBO ART
Mask of a female ancestral spirit
19th century.
Painted wood; height 12".

ritual product with a fixed theme representing a symbol of fertility in the shape of the antelope, mother and child. It can only be understood if one imagines it as it was worn, by a dancer who fixed it to his head over wig-like fibers of tree bark. Even though a late version, it preserves, in the double stance of the legs and in the sinuous, vertical rhythm of the upper part — ending in high spiral horns above the lace-like stylizations of the fur — an elegance and a movement which derive from a highly developed tradition, particularly skilled in vertical compositions.

BALSOBO ART. *Mask of a Female Ancestral Spirit.*
This mask was used in the dances of the Mukui, a very powerful woman's secret society of the Balsobo tribe, from the forests of Western Gabon. There are different types of masks of this kind, all of which combine accurately observed facial expressions with a complete stylization of lines and forms. This mask is conceived according to a rigorously frontal plan, with all its parts symmetrically arranged within an ovoid outline. The arresting humorous character of the expression is brought out most forcefully by the stylized motif of the double arches of eyes and eyebrows, between the two horizontal lines at nose and forehead.

23

BENIN ART
Two leopards
Probably 19th century.
Ivory and copper;
length 31 1/2".

ASHANTI ART
Akua Iba Doll
19th–20th century.
Wood; height 11 3/4".

ASHANTI ART. *Akua Iba Doll.*

This is an example of a ritual object to ensure fertility and good health for children. It is used by the agricultural and matriarchal population of the Ashanti, in Ghana. The Ashanti also produce brass sculpture, with figures of birds, fish and other animals. The style of this doll has many elements in common with terra cottas of the Baule tribe. Though following a certain fixed formula, these dolls are not mass produced; there is a large number of them, within which we find many variants and different interpretations. Each doll is made up of a large flat or hollow disc, often with engravings on the back, and in front, a face in relief. The neck is geometrically stylized; from the conical torso emerge the crutchlike arms and rounded shapes alluding to the natural functions of fertility.

These strange sculptures are outstanding among African arts because of their extraordinary abstract, contemplative character.

BENIN ART. *Two Leopards.*

These works are owned by Queen Elizabeth II and are on loan to the British Museum. Each of the animals is made of five pieces of elephant tusk; it is thus a luxury item destined for the court. Like bronze sculptors, ivory carvers in the Kingdom of Benin formed a special caste, whose tradition lasted even after the end of the state. These two leopards, which can be dated to the nineteenth century, are composed in an imposing monumental

24

style. Their bodies are decorated with a finely worked relief pattern of a beaded texture, surrounding the larger, copper plaques which give the surface a slower, more regular rhythm. The patterns converge towards the animals' heads, with ears erect and jaws half-open. The artist has penetrated into the character of these wild animals; both their hidden energy and the splendor of their pelts have been transfigured. This and other remarkable works serve to prove the high level of civilization maintained in Nigeria by the people of Ife and Benin through the course of at least seven centuries.

MELANESIAN ART. *Amulet.*

This sculpture, too, presents a crystallization of an earlier model, probably archaic. Because of its use in magic, great importance is given to the head as the seat of the spirit; in comparison, note the summarily rendered arms. The tapering of the form both below and above may have been dictated by the function of the figure as a blunt instrument for working destructive magic. The artist's attention was concentrated on the head and face, which is summarized in abstract arches for the eyes and a depression for the mouth, echoed by the curve of the nose and of the hairline. The elliptical composition, linear and sculptural at the same time, unifies this work within a powerfully expressive intensity, especially in the fantastic extension and development of the head.

SEPIK ART. *Figure of a Crouching Woman.*

Among the many traditions and styles peculiar to New Guinea is the so-called Korwal style, to be found in the northwestern Geelvink Bay. It includes, along with many other motifs, both realistic and abstract, a group of stylized open-work figures and seated personages. The artist of the

MELANESIAN ART
Amulet
19th century.
Carved stone; height 9 1/8".

SEPIK ART
Figure of a crouching woman
Beginning of 20th century.
Painted wood, glass eyes;
height 9 1/4".

crouching female illustrated here has followed a refined criterion of sculptural composition. Within the cylindrical form which limits its dimensions, the artist has carved a figure on two opposed diagonals, the one of the face above, and the one of the knees below. The wild vitality of the figure is thus contained in its own unity and rhythmic balance, from the feet which grasp the decorated base to the almost disconcertingly intent face.

MAORI ART.   *Urn Cover of a Tribal Chief.*

This is a remarkable example of funerary Maori sculpture. The Maoris emigrated to New Zealand in about the thirteenth century and were discovered in 1799 by Captain Cook. Until 1871, when they made peace with the white settlers, they jealously preserved their own cultural and artistic identity, which still exists. The characteristics of form and decoration to be

MAORI ART
Urn cover of a tribal chief
19th–20th century.
Carved and incised wood.

noted in this figure relate to those of all Maori productions: huts, canoes, coffins (made in the shape of a body), staffs and other instruments and objects. This piece continues an old tradition of clearly intelligible, realist form included in a composition of balanced, carefully distributed elements, animated by an all-over pattern of engraved surface decoration. Most evident is the spiral motif, together with other undulating and radiating motifs which were also used for tattoos. The execution, particularly of the head, shows an exquisitely sensitive sense of the material.

ZUNI ART
Vase with deer
19th century.
Terra cotta, painted in red and blue-black;
height 10 1/4";
diameter 12".

ZUÑI ART.   *Vase with Deer.*

Among the many ceramic forms which the Zuñi Indians of the American Southwest used for their water vases, this is one of the most interesting because of its excellent preservation and high style. The artist operated freely within a traditional repertory, and the decoration, painted between the bands which define the neck and the body of the vase, were executed with evident spontaneity. This is particularly evident in the figure of the deer inside their little "houses" of stylized arches. Each animal is individualized, with a life and vitality of its own; even the X-ray section connecting mouth to stomach, which is symbolic, is rendered by a flexible, sweeping line. The frieze compositions of the lower panels, including a procession of double-tailed birds, show a love for elaborated and contrasting geometric pattern.

HAIDA ART
Chest for clothes and jewelry
19th century.
Wood inlaid with shells
and animal tusks.

HAIDA ART.   *Chest for Clothes and Jewelry.*

This object is believed to come from the culture of the Haida tribe of Queen Charlotte Island off the northwest coast of North America, a tribe famous for its carved wood work in houses, totems, furniture, boxes, etc. The figured motifs relate to tribal symbolism. This example shows a large figure, perhaps a bear, containing a smaller, human figure. Symmetrically arranged on either side of this central frontal element are curving profiles of animals, probably fish. The artist systematically disconnects all the parts, which are then distributed over a surface divided into three identical sections. The two sides have an exact rhythmic correspondence, the patterns being reversed so they face the center. The symmetry of the composition casts a spell and adds to the fascinating effect of this strange work.

AZTEC ART.   *Xipe-Totec, God of Spring and Fertility.*   pp. 30–31

This was a mask, used in ceremonies in which a man believed to be the incarnation of the god was killed. His flayed skin was worn by a priest: for this reason, on other similar masks, there are two open mouths, as for a double face. The hard stone, difficult to work, is carved with such technical skill as to attain a sculptural form of extraordinary purity; notice the flowing rhythm of the curved lines of the profiles, and the modeling of the re-

lief. The decoration on the back is magic and religious in character; it is also strongly stylized. The mask itself in its stark simplicity represents the high attainment of the Aztec masters, a result of long experience and consciousness of form.

MIXTEC ART. *Souche Nuttar Codex.*   *pp. 32–33*

This illuminated book depicts the origins of the royal family and the submission of tribes. The sheets illustrated on pp. 32–33 represent the origins of the family of the chief Tirantongo; various incidents and episodes, dating back perhaps to the seventh century; and a hero of the Mixtec tribe who has won a battle. Above the main figures are smaller ones, like hieroglyphs, symbolizing years and names. The custom of using the tanned hides of deer and other animals to make illuminated manuscripts started in the twelfth century; these codices, besides being a priceless instrument for the reconstruction of the history of the peoples of the Mexican plateau, are, like the frescoes, typical of a great artistic expression. The miniatures are drawn in a linear style with elastic, well-defined lines which are sometimes repeated and filled in with various colors. The drawing is in profile and two-dimensional. The subject matter is indicated in ritual gestures and in the magnificence of ceremonial costume. A strong rhythmic and coloristic effect is achieved, both in the isolated figures and in the compositions of facing couples, as well as in the stylized figures of animals and in the decorative details.

Left and **right:**
AZTEC ART
Mask of
Xipe-Totec, God of Spring and Fertility
14th century
Basalt, carved on both sides;
10″ × 11 7/8″.

MIXTEC ART
Souche Nuttar Codex
14th century (?).
Drawing and painting on deerskin;
the codex has 48 sheets;
total length 48";
each sheet 7" × 10".

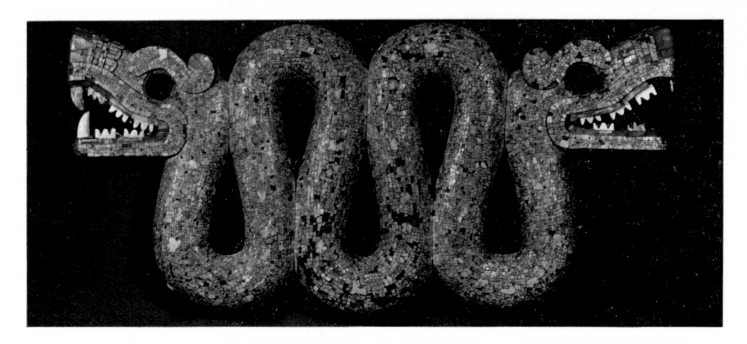

AZTEC OR MIXTEC ART. *Two-Headed Serpent.*

This mosaic work of precious stones, probably a breast-plate, comes from Monte Alban, where many examples of Mixtec handiwork — metalwork, gems, mosaics — have been found in the excavations. These works were exported by the commercial Pochetas into the country of the Mayas and elsewhere. This object is characterized by the controlled development of the serpentine line between the two vividly colored animal heads.

AZTEC ART. *Skull-Mask of the God Tezcatlipoca.*

The mask is believed to represent Tezcatlipoca, god of the emptiness of night, particularly honored at Texcoco. A decorated skull probably comes from a human sacrifice; the tradition of a skull as an image has lasted in Mexico until today. The Aztec artist followed the structure of the skeleton and preserved its teeth, but he also applied the criterion of decorative transformation that is found in other masks, dividing the face into alternating light and dark zones and reducing to pure forms the eye-sockets and nasal cavity. The mask thus loses its funerary aspect and becomes an extraordinary sculptured, visual figure.

TLINGIT–HAIDA ART. *Hawk.*   *p. 36*

This fine sculpture was made by a Tlingit-Haida Indian from the northwest coast of North America. There are many wood sculptures, paintings, textiles, embroidery and woven baskets of this culture. Their peculiar types and forms, which have a long tradition, have a wide repertory, which often presents a complicated symbolism. This hawk, for example, evidently renders a number of intellectualized concepts by means of stylization. Both mass and surface are treated this way. The structure of the sculpture is expressed in terms of volumes, while the carefully divided zones of the surface are marked off by sharply defined lines, as well as by alternation or contrast of colors. The resulting effect is one of conscious magnificence.

AZTEC OR MIXTEC ART
Two-headed serpent
15th century.
Turquoise and shells
set on a wooden frame;
width 17 1/2".

AZTEC ART
Skull-mask of the God Tezcatlipoca
15th–16th century.
Human skull covered with mosaic
of turquoise and obsidian;
eyes of polished pieces of pyrite;
height 6 3/4".

On page 36:
TLINGIT–HAIDA ART
Hawk
19th century.
Painted wood.

34

ANCIENT EGYPT

PREDYNASTIC EGYPTIAN ART. *Box from El Amrah.*

The second "culture," named after the site of Nagada in Upper Egypt, where the archeological material typical of this civilization was found, represents the final phase of Egyptian prehistory, which was followed by the historic or "dynastic" epochs. It is believed that the people who carried this culture came into the Nile Valley from the Red Sea by way of the Hammamat River and settled in Upper Egypt, from where they spread southward along the Nile. There they apparently introduced the art of writing and the techniques of irrigation, as well as the use of rectangular dwellings instead of round huts. "Nagada II" pottery, which consists of vases in a variety of shapes and, exceptionally, rectangular boxes like this one, is characterized by its red-brown decoration, with figures of boats, animals and plants on a whitish or beige background. The box reproduced below has the characteristic motifs of a boat, groups of fish snapping at a fish-hook — neither seen in this view — and a group of four animals, believed to represent Kudu gazelles or antelopes, walking along on a line representing the ground. The fresh naturalism with which the slender figures of these beasts are sketched points to a connection with the prehistoric incised and painted rock art of the Tassili region. It is difficult for us today to understand the meaning of the horizontal comb-like lines, or of those in the shape of straight and reversed "S"s added to the composition. Are they simply abstract motifs filling empty spaces; a primitive avoidance of the blank? Or are they intended to represent a landscape of trees, grass and water, in a very stylized manner? Probably one alternative does not exclude the other, and perhaps these double combs and straight and reversed "S" signs had already attained a fixed conventional meaning in the pictorial phases preceding a fully developed system of ideograms. In this case, the association of landscape symbols with the figures can be explained both on the basis of the rhythm of the appearance, that is, of an esthetic composition, as well as on their literal meanings.

EGYPTIAN ART, OLD KINGDOM
Katep and his wife
Dynasty IV (2723–2563 B.C.).
Painted limestone; height 18 3/4".
From el Amrah.

PREDYNASTIC EGYPTIAN ART
Box
End of the second period of Nagda
(second half of IV millennium B.C.).
Painted terra cotta;
reproduced about actual size.
From el Amrah.

EGYPTIAN ART, OLD KINGDOM
Statue of the shipbuilder Pejemes
Dynasty III (2778–2723 B.C.).
Pink granite; height 25 1/4".
From el Gizeh.

EGYPTIAN ART, MIDDLE KINGDOM
Head of Amenemhat III
Dynasty XII (1991–1786 B.C.).
Granite; height 31 1/2".
From Bubastis on the Delta.

EGYPTIAN ART, THE OLD KINGDOM.   *Katep and His Wife.*   p. 39
The funerary group of Katep and his wife, found in a private tomb in the
shape of a *mastaba* (or truncated pyramid) at el Gizeh, in the sepulchral
area of ancient Memphis, is an example of the non-official art of "common-
ers" of the time of the Great Pyramids. We are still, however, within the
stylistic context of court art, to which belong the statues or groups dedicated
to persons of a higher rank. In spite of a certain lack of proportion in the
bodies — i.e. the large heads and short necks — both figures appear
blocked out in their essential volumes like the statues of the Pharaohs. Even
though the woman's arm embraces her husband's wrist, both statues are
conceived separately. Both are frontal, but can be seen from any of four
views, front, back, right and left: the original block has been worked, as it
were, on each of these four faces.

EGYPTIAN ART, THE OLD KINGDOM.   *Statue of the Shipbuilder
Pejemes.*

The seated statue of the shipbuilder Pejemes, shown holding an axe on his
shoulder, is one of the earliest statues of private individuals existing, in the
British Museum and elsewhere. The use of very hard granite, instead of leading the artist to the most simplified and architectural geometry characteristic
of the statues of Pharaohs in the Old Kingdom, seems here to have led him
to abandon the figure at a stage that seems to correspond to a sketch, to the
first blocking-out rather than to the final formal statue. On the other hand,
if we compare it to the only preserved contemporaneous statue of a
Pharaoh, that is of the III Dynasty King Zoser in the Cairo Museum, we
can see that they have many elements in common: the naturalistic heads
and the limbs kept in the compact cube of the block. The most obvious
differences appear to be due to the less careful attention paid to proportions by the commoner craftsmen, who were freer than artists working on
monumental royal works. During this phase, stone statuary seems still to
preserve a vivid memory of an early "totemic" phase, when it was sufficient
simply to add some distinctive attribute to the vertical pole — column or
stone — to make it acceptable as a representation of the human figure.
The artist was somehow in a more favorable position, as compared to the
more classical periods, to appreciate the positive values in the unfinished
look.

EGYPTIAN ART, MIDDLE KINGDOM.   *Head of Amenemhat III.*
Though this head is mutilated, it has lost none of its extraordinarily expres-
sive quality. This fragment, which has been identified as a portrait of
Amenemhat III, originally belonged to a colossal seated figure placed,
with another, identical statue, in the eastern part of the temple at Bubastis.
The British Museum also owns an important fragment of the body.
Amenemhat III reigned during almost half a century, toward the end of the
Twelfth Dynasty. He had a strong personality as a builder and as a ruler.
Many of his predecessors were strong rulers, too; they raised the fortunes
of the state during the relatively brief span of the Middle Kingdom. This

portrait consciously reflects the stylistic models of the Old Kingdom, but also appears to express, by means of the severe, concentrated representation of the features, the inner qualities of the king. It shows the ability to search deeply into the human soul, an ability that the sculptors of the Middle Kingdom possessed to a degree attained at no other time in ancient Eastern art.

EGYPTIAN ART, MIDDLE KINGDOM. *Funerary Mask of a Lady with the Attributes of Isis.*

Embalming corpses was practiced since very remote times. Actual mummification developed later, probably only during the Middle Kingdom. The process aimed to preserve not only the corporeal substance, but also the features of the dead. That was the purpose also of making an anthropomorphic sarcophagus and of paying special attention to the part covering the face. This "mask," therefore, particularly in the oldest examples, aims at an even fuller realism than that of the statues themselves.

The use of precious material or its imitation in painting, on the other hand, had the purpose of going beyond mere realism, which was, sublimated as it were, into sacred goldwork. In this piece, the gilding — gold dust on varnish — and the vivid blue-green color of hair, eyes and eyebrows simulate the contrast of solid gold inlaid with enamel, materials used, for example, in the much later sarcophagus of Tut-ankh-amon.

EGYPTIAN ART, SECOND INTERMEDIATE PERIOD. *Sarcophagus of the Pharaoh Iniotep.*

Parallel to the XVIth Dynasty of the later Hyksos, who maintained their rule on the Delta during the period from about 1630 to 1580 B.C., there also ruled, probably since 1680 B.C., the independent dynasty of the lords of Thebes.

Iniotep's face, as it appears in the "mask" of the wooden sarcophagus, after the almost total loss of gilding, is marked by a vivid realism, emphasized by the intensity of the metal and obsidian eyes, still in perfect condition. This realistic feeling was certainly not the effect of the original, when it was taken from the workshop, polished and gilded to perfection; yet it reflects the expressive intent of the artist, who remembered the deep psychological interest of the sculptures of the Middle Kingdom.

EGYPTIAN ART OF THE NEW KINGDOM. *Colossal Statue of Rameses II.*
p. 44

During the XVIIIth Dynasty (1580–1314 B.C.), Egypt, after having been a vassal of the Hyksos, became a world power. Following the unsuccessful reforms of Amenhotep III — Akhenaten — it underwent severe religious and political crises. This is the "Amarna" period, so called from the modern

Salt

Amarna, which corresponds to the site of Tell-el-Amarna, the mysterious capital of the heretic pharaoh.

The following dynasty re-established the old worship, but did not succeed in re-establishing completely its earlier absolute power.

During the 67 years of the reign of Rameses II, the third pharaoh of that dynasty, art had an incomparable development, at least in regard to quantity. This is true for all of Egypt, but more particularly for the two great cult sites of ancient Thebes now called by the names of their modern villages, Luxor and Karnak. Thebes was no longer the court capital or a center of the administration, but it remained a religious and cultural capital. From Karnak comes this colossus, bearing on its shoulders the king's titles. Similar colossal statues, frequent among the works ordered by Rameses II, were more symbolic than representational, and they seem to have been almost mass produced. The hieratic stylization of the older production was once more taken up, but with an elegant, refined and "mannered" interpretation, which can only be explained by the influence of the intervening Amarna style.

EGYPTIAN ART OF THE NEW KINGDOM. *Statue of Senmut, Minister of Queen Hatshepsut.*

The motif of a personage seated on the ground with folded arms on knees, the whole body included within the limits of a cubic block, appears in Egyptian funerary sculpture since the Middle Kingdom. It is still a favorite pose during the Late Period and even in Ptolemaic art. The figure of the deceased is shown in the act of receiving the funerary offerings; these were evidently, at least originally, deposited on the horizontal plane of the folded arms.

In this case we have Senmut, an official and minister of Queen Hatshepsut. It seems strange therefore that this work, which shows some analogies with contemporary "folk" sculpture, does not reach the severe style of the similar, contemporary statue of Sennefer, also in the British Museum. Perhaps, though, it is not possible fully to appreciate it because of the damaged condition of mouth and nose. This may even be due to an attempt at reworking and improving the face.

EGYPTIAN ART, NEW KINGDOM. *Wine Jar of Painted Terra Cotta.*

p. 46

Ceramics did not play an important role in the development of Egyptian art. Only in the New Kingdom did the beauty and variety of smooth, wheel-turned forms bring some prestige even to terra cotta containers of more or less common use. Such is the case with this wine jar, sometimes called "amphora," but incorrectly since it does not have handles. It has light blue painted decorations, with a motif of lotus petals distributed in three zones and a dedicatory inscription. Vases of metal or alabaster were preferred for ceremonial use, nevertheless the elegance of the tapering lines of this once commonplace vase and its bell-shaped cover are admirable, as is the simple, almost Greek rhythm of the decoration.

EGYPTIAN ART, NEW KINGDOM.   *Necklace.*

The manufacture of vitreous glazes seems to go back to predynastic Egypt. The glass was obtained by heating a mixture of sand together with ash or a natural carbonate of sodium. It was never transparent, but could easily be colored, at least by the beginning of the New Kingdom. At first, the only colors derived from copper, that is, green and blue; then white, yellow and red were added. The blue always remained in use because of its effectiveness in small pieces. This necklace from el Amarna represents the product of a workshop active at the time of Akhenaten. It corresponds closely to the usual type of the New Kingdom, often represented in reliefs and paintings of the time: three circles of leaves and petals are disposed radially and connected by four strings of beads, joined at the ends to two lotus-shaped pieces. Kings and queens probably preferred to wear more costly necklaces of hard stones set in gold, which became the models for these fine glass pieces.

EGYPTIAN ART, NEW KINGDOM.   *Container in the Shape of a Fish.*

This little fish-shaped vase made of many-colored glass, one of the masterpieces of ancient glass manufacture, probably comes from the same Amarna workshop which produced the necklace illustrated above. The process by which similar containers were obtained, since glass blowing was not known, seems to have been the following: the form of the interior of the vase was modeled with a rather loose material such as a mixture of clay and a larger amount of sand. This form was stuck to one end of a metal pole and dipped into a crucible, where the glass chosen for the basic color — in this case dark blue — was melting; it was then removed, coated with a layer of a uniform thickness. Before this sticky crust could get cold, they applied to it long, pulled-out pieces of different colors, which had been stretched and kept in a semi-fluid state. A pointed or comb-shaped instrument drawn across the body added the characteristic wave-like movement.

The external surface was smoothed and cooled. The inner core, easily crumbled, was finally extracted from the mouth of the container. In the course of successive applications and heating other details could be added, such as, in this case, the fins and tail.

EGYPTIAN ART, NEW KINGDOM.   *Fragment of a Fresco: Cattle Inspection.*   *pp. 48–49*

Egyptian wall painting seems to presuppose models in the form of pen drawings, perhaps in illustrated manuscripts, colored with transparent paints.

In mural painting, this process was inverted, since otherwise the colors would have covered or dimmed the contours. First the form was drawn and

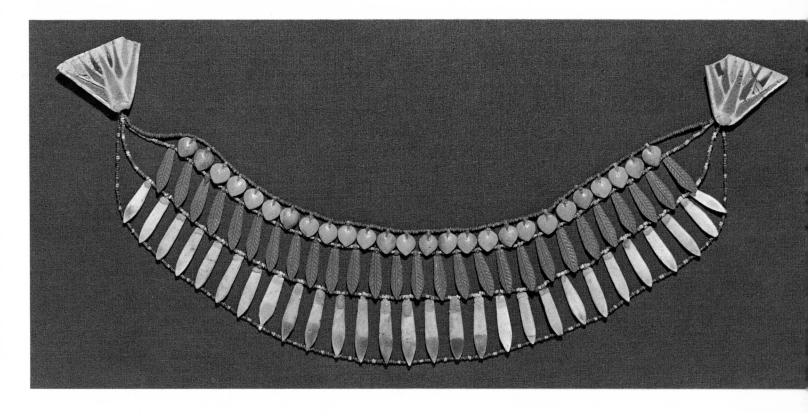

EGYPTIAN ART, NEW KINGDOM
Necklace
Dynasty XVIII (ca. 1370–1350 B.C.).
Glass paste.
From Tell el Amarna.

EGYPTIAN ART, NEW KINGDOM
Wine jar
Dynasty XVIII (ca. 1370 B.C.).
Painted terra cotta; height 31 1/4".

EGYPTIAN ART, NEW KINGDOM
Container in the shape of a fish
Dynasty XVIII (ca. 1370–1350 B.C.).
Glass; length 5 1/2".
From Tell el Amarna.

On pages 48–49:
EGYPTIAN ART, NEW KINGDOM
Cattle inspection
Dynasty XVIII (1580–1314 B.C.).
Fragment of a fresco.
Dimensions of the whole fragment:
45 1/4" × 15 3/4".
From a tomb at Thebes.

filled in with color, and only then were the contours drawn; this process can be noted in several unfinished paintings.

The result of this is that, during the execution, the fresco was much more "painting" and much less "colored drawing" than would appear at the end of the work. In this case, although the artist did not aim consciously at effects of light and shade, and only attempted to render realistically the various shades of the spotted and dappled bodies of the oxen, the result is actually three dimensional. The oxen are seen in the round; they have been painted as living animals, modeled by the light, not as skins flattened out on a tanner's frame. This is true in spite of the fact that the problem of light is avoided: its source is not indicated; there are no cast shadows. Yet the third dimension is introduced, at least in the foreheads of each of the animals; and even the overlapping perspective of the figures achieves an original, realistic significance.

EGYPTIAN ART, NEW KINGDOM. *Banquet Scene.*

Above the detail illustrated here, not shown in this reproduction, we see spectators, watching the spectacle. In spite of the sharp division of the black line separating the two zones, it seems certain that everything included in the upper area is intended to be *behind* what appears in the lower register. The dancers and the players, in other words, must be understood to be on a stage in the foreground, the audience in the back. In this composition all the Egyptian conventions seem to be respected. The same is true in respect to the representation of the various parts of the body, thus an eye appears frontally in a profile face, or we have a front view of a torso while the arms and legs are shown in profile. The only exceptions to this rule are the two central figures, the girl playing the double flute, and the other beating time with joined hands like her two companions at her left (or performing a static hand dance, as is still done today in Java or Bali). It is

EGYPTIAN ART, NEW KINGDOM
Banquet scene
Dynasty XVIII (1580–1314 B.C.).
Detail of a fragment from a wall painting.
Dimensions of the whole fragment:
27 1/4″ × 11 3/4″.
From the tomb of a certain Nebamon at Thebes.

clear that the frontal view of a face was not inconceivable for an Egyptian artist: it was, however, usually avoided, because in an outline drawing a lateral view of the nose is almost necessary, as we see even in the present case. The inclusion of a nose in profile within a frontal face, although really neither less nor more credible than the usual frontal eye in a profile face, was nevertheless not a part of the accepted repertory, standardized ever since the time of the first dynasties. Having introduced it in this case implies on the part of the artist a remarkable courage. Innovations of this kind, however, were destined to remain isolated, or rather marginal attempts, since to persist in them would in the end mean trying totally to revise all accepted conventions. This in practice would be unthinkable as long as the indispensable ideographic writing imposed certain visual "models" endowed with an essential and privileged "truth."

EGYPTIAN ART, NEW KINGDOM. *Garden with Fish Pond.*

When from a window we watch a procession of people in the street, especially a parade taking place in two rows, rather far apart, the impression received by the retina will be quite similar to that seen in certain Egyptian frescoes: the street looks something like a map, and the two ranks will appear one above the other. But the superimposed, well ordered, neat registers of Egyptian painting represent in fact a conventionalized autonomy of their own. Each section by itself conforms to its principal viewpoint — like a line of soldiers, a row of trees — but can also be freely combined with other "views" or "registers." So, in representations of gardens, where there are four rows of trees at the sides of the swimming pool, these may be

On page 54:
EGYPTIAN ART, ROMAN PERIOD
Portrait of Artemidorus
2nd century A.D.
Upper part of a mummy covering.
Wax painted on wood; height 12 5/8".
From el Fayum (?).

EGYPTIAN ART, NEW KINGDOM
Garden with fish pond
Dynasty XVIII (1580–1314 B.C.).
Fragment of decoration
of a tomb at Thebes.
Fresco, 28 3/8" × 24 1/4".

shown as on a map, to add to the accuracy of the representation. A combined view is not permitted, because it confuses the individual elements. In some cases all four rows are turned toward the exterior, like the four walls of a room. In other cases, as here, the short vertical sides are collapsed to the outside, while the long sides are arranged in registers; which means that what is "in back" is painted "above." The "lower register" is, furthermore, pushed down so that the foliage of the trees will not hide the pool. We do not know, in this case, whether there actually were trees on the right. Yet we can still admire the decorative elegance of this "map" of a country estate at Thebes, and the precise realism with which the fish, the water-lilies and the birds in the pool have been depicted. There is even a realistically humorous note in the prim gait of the two geese and the awkward flapping of the ducks.

EGYPTIAN ART, LATE PERIOD. *Sarcophagus from Thebes.*
Starting with the XXth Dynasty we find anthropomorphic or "mummy-shaped" sarcophagi of wood, or modeled out of a mixture of chalk, glue and vegetable fibres, completely painted, inside and out, with scenes taken from the *Book of the Dead*. These scenes are often, as in the present case, carefully framed by formal decorations and ornamental divisions, and symmetrically placed on the body of the sarcophagus. Within the individual scenes, the placement of figures and decorative elements shows the same search for symmetry and the same clearly defined compositions as does the general plan of the decorations of the sarcophagus; all of this being carried out with considerable technical skill.

EGYPTIAN ART, ROMAN PERIOD. *Portrait of Artemidorus.* p. 54
During the Roman period the practice of embalming spread to people other than the Egyptians and continued to be used by the Hellenized classes of the native population. In this period the sarcophagus was often substituted by a rigid covering, which was sometimes shaped, stuccoed and painted so as to simulate a sarcophagus.

On the face were placed either real wood or *papier-mâché* masks painted and gilded, or portraits painted with wax or tempera on wood or canvas. These are practically the only remaining documents of Graeco-Roman easel painting; they are named after the oasis of el Fayum, where the greatest number were found.

There are two styles: one, entirely in the Hellenistic tradition, is realistic and pictorial; the other, which in the end prevailed, turned once more to a two dimensional, "expressionistic," schematic system. The second, which was technically inferior, already foreshadowed the styles of late antiquity. The portrait of Artemidorus, even though it is not one of the most classical, nevertheless belongs to the first category. The face is modeled by means of a strong chiaroscuro relief, and the wax (or encaustic) color succeeds in rendering the brilliance of the eyes and the shine of the skin. The decoration of the covering, which goes back to old Pharaonic models, seems to reflect the "antique," "classic" taste of a Greek workshop, more than to imply any continuation of the ancient Egyptian tradition.

EGYPTIAN ART, LATE PERIOD
Sarcophagus
Dynasties XXII–XXV
(around 9th–8th century B.C.).
painted wood; height 77 1/4".
From Thebes.

ANCIENT NEAR EAST

ART OF PREHISTORIC IRAN. *Decorated Vase.*

In the first half of the fourth millennium B.C., parallel to the Sumerian culture there developed beyond the Zagros Mountains, in Western Iran, a special culture which is called Susa I. This culture precedes the Proto-Elamite phase and is characterized, above all, by the high level of its pottery. There are wheel-made bowls, cups and vases with thin walls, decorated in a dark brown color on a white-yellowish background. The Louvre has an even larger collection of pottery belonging to this period, also from Susa. This piece, however, is one of the most remarkable examples in the whole group because of the balance and harmony with which its geometric decorations are distributed. The shape is a truncated cone; except for the band of stylized birds encircling the upper rim of the vase, only geometric forms appear: stripes, lines and vertical, horizontal or zigzag bands, lozenges and triangles. It is possible that such signs might have a symbolic meaning. According to one opinion (Yoshikawa), the zigzag bands may represent the four rivers springing out from the mountains, signified by the black triangles alternating with the group of birds at the four cardinal points. This would be a prehistoric anticipation of the late myth of the four rivers of Paradise.

In that case, the decreasing triangles disposed in the vertical sections could also be mountain chains, stylized according to the models of vertical overlapping of forms. Even if we do not understand all the possible symbols, we can still admire the decorative vigor of this piece.

SUMERIAN ART, PROTODYNASTIC PERIOD. *Standard of Ur: Peace, detail.*

The *Standard of Ur* is so titled because it has been thought that it might have been fixed on a pole to serve as a processional standard; its actual use is not really known. The decoration is similar to that of the frame of certain harps which have been found in great number in the same royal cemetery of ancient Ur.

It comes from a princely tomb. The objects that have been found with it seem to be prior to the time of those dynasts who can be identified with certainty. This agrees with the findings in the tomb of a certain Meskalamdu, not otherwise known but supposed to have been a king immediately preceding those dynasts in date, that is, at the beginning of the Ur I period. This is the final phase of the protodynastic period (end of IV millennium — ca. 2460 B.C.) in Ur, parallel to the flourishing of the ancient Shurupak (modern Fara) and the best known phase of that culture.

This is a flat casket, decorated on all four sides with inlaid figures. The material is chiefly shells for the figures and lapis-lazuli for the backgrounds; red limestone appears on the borders. The two larger sides show, in three registers, two ample compositions, seemingly related to a specific event and celebrating a victory. On one side are the actual battles. On the other, we see the king, wearing a fur skirt and drinking with his family or people of

ART OF PREHISTORIC IRAN
Vase decorated with geometric motifs and stylized birds
"Susa I" period
(first half of 4th millennium B.C.).
Painted terra cotta; height 8″.
From Susa.

the court in the upper register: these personages are also seated on elegant chairs. In the lower register the conquered people bring him tribute. The scenes on the two panels are known respectively as *War* and *Peace*.

Our reproduction shows a large section of the left half of the latter. Here the artist uses the difficult technique of inlay. Frontal perspective is strictly respected: the eyes are shown frontally, as in Egypt, and even seated figures, if represented in profile, have both feet visible. In spite of this the scene has a lively naturalism, a narrative vitality we seldom find in ancient art and which has some relationship to modern cartoon drawings. Notice for instance the king's satisfied face as he drinks, and the glowering porter in the lower section.

These achievements are made possible by an exceptionally well defined outline, obtained by the use of contrasting black bitumen inlaid into the shallowly carved white shell background.

LATE SUMERIAN ART
Portrait of Gudea (?)
Upper part of male statue.
Period of Gudea (ca. 2290–2255 B.C.).
Diorite, with traces of gilt on the nails;
height 30 1/4".
Probably from Telloh
(ancient Girsu, near Lagash).

LATE SUMERIAN ART.   *Portrait of Gudea* (?).

After the interruption of the Akkadian domination of Sargon ("Shar-ruukin") and his successors, which lasted less than two centuries, the Sumerian cities gradually regained their autonomy and a part of their previous political power. The first to regain power were the *ensi* (kings, rulers) of Lagash: this period derives its name from Gudea, the main personality of the time. The art of the period of Gudea follows the traditions of the Akkadian dynasty, which introduces a freer and more naturalistic concept of both the human figure and narrative relief. This art, however, is almost exclusively limited to subjects of worship and to votive statues, either seated or standing.

We have many statues of Gudea himself, shown at prayer. Identified by inscriptions, they are carved mostly out of diorite, a hard, black, shining stone. The fragment of a statue shown here has no inscription and therefore cannot be identified with certainty — the physical resemblance is not significant, as other rulers, too, have similar features — but it is among the most remarkable of the group for the precision and modeling of its volumes.

It may be thought that the sculptors of this time, having to work with a very hard stone, which was, indeed, imported, would profit from Egyptian experience in this field. Though their ample, geometric shapes might have some resemblance with Pharaonic sculpture, there is nothing in these humble and human mortals who pray to their god to remind us of the proud detachment of the Pharaoh, the "living god."

SYRIAN ART.   *Seated Statue of King Idrimi*.   *p. 60*

The statue originally included two basalt lions, which are now broken, on both sides of the throne. It was dedicated by Idrimi in the temple of Alalakh, capital of the Mukish country, which previously was subject to a wider Kingdom whose capital was Halab (present day Aleppo). He dedicated this statue after thirty years of reign, having been placed on the throne as a vassal by the Mitannian king Paradarna. Earlier, Idrimi, whose family had been dethroned from Halab by a rebellion, had lived adventurously, as we are told by the long inscription which covers the statue

Although it shows some influence from Sumer, as in the crouching position and in the staring eyes, the statue also has Anatolian or Phoenician elements, for example the prominence of the head and its tapered, "corkscrew" shape, unusual in Mesopotamian art.

PHOENICIAN ART.   *Ivory Inlay Representing a Lioness Mauling a Nubian.*
This ivory piece, whose Phoenician origin has been proven, was found in a well under room NN of the Northwest Palace of Assurnasipal II (883–859 B.C.), in the ancient Assyrian city of Kalhu, together with other ivory fragments and a similar plaque, now in the Baghdad Museum. It was a fragment of the decoration of a throne or some other important piece of furniture, dating from the latest renovation of the palace, under the reign of Sargon II (721–705 B.C.).

Many inlaid precious stones and part of the gold foil are lost, but even in its present condition it is possible to appreciate the extraordinary richness of the piece.

The Phoenician artist imitates the stylized figures of Egyptian goldsmiths in his floral decoration, and reminds us of Egyptian art even in the ancient symbolism showing the Pharaoh as a lion defeating his enemy, and in the reflections of Amarna style in the Nubian's face. What is astonishing, however, is that the artist could attain such a tender and sensual naturalism and be able to conceive the prostrate figure in such a "life-like" position, completely unknown to the conventional schemes of the time.

PHOENICIAN ART
*Ivory inlay representing a lioness mauling
a Nubian in a papyrus bush.*
721–705 B.C.
Ivory with gold foil and inlaid gold,
lapsis-lazuli and carnelian;
reproduced about actual size.
From Kalhu
("Calah," known today as Nimrud).

61

ASSYRIAN ART. *King Assurbanipal's Lion Hunt.*

The "Imperial" art of the Late Assyrian period, which inherited motifs
from the preceding Mesopotamian cultures but was also open to other influences, returned to the narrative relief. Assyrian sculptors, when celebrating their kings' military achievements, sometimes became accurate chroni-
clers rather than creators, using formulae borrowed from neighbors.

On the other hand they created imposing original figures of gods, demons
and kings. In these, the juxtaposition of different perspectives — such as
the use of a frontal eye in profiles — and the stylization of details of the
anatomy and garments — such as sharply defined muscles or folds in relief — does not prevent the emergence of strong volumes and structures
conceived naturalistically, almost like a prelude to archaic Greek art.

ASSYRIAN ART
King Assurbanipal's lion hunt
Ca. 650 B.C.
Alabaster relief, originally painted;
height of plaque 66"
From Nineveh

The highest achievements of Assyrian sculpture, however, are found in
animal scenes, particularly in the large panels of *Assurbanipal's Hunt* (668–
629 B.C.). These were sculptured in relief on alabaster as decoration of at
least two rooms in the Northern Palace in Nineveh, built by this king around
the middle of the century: most of the reliefs were discovered in 1854 and
transferred to the British Museum.

The composition is set on a bare background; the spatial relationships
succeed in attaining naturalistic effects; the animal figures, great vitality.

On pages 64–65:
ASSYRIAN ART
Dying lioness
Ca. 650 B.C.
Detail from the *Royal Hunt of Assurbanipal.*
Alabaster relief, originally painted;
height of detail, 15 3/4″.
From Nineveh.

ASSYRIAN ART. *Dying Lioness.*   *pp. 64–65*

This is deservedly one of the most admired sections of *Assurbanipal's Hunt.*
It represents a mortally wounded lioness: though her spine is broken by the

arrows and she drags her paralyzed back legs, yet she roars out, raising her head against her persecutors.

The ferocious and yet pathetic expression of the dying beast could not be obtained by mechanical, conventional formulae. As a matter of fact these achievements imply a very mature interest in reality and a skill in perspective; notice the perfection of the eye, nostril and mouth. To a modern observer it is difficult to believe that this same artist still could put frontal eyes on a human profile.

IRANIAN ART OF THE ACHAEMENIAN PERIOD. *Gold Bracelet.*
Decorated with two dragons, this gold bracelet is the richest and most impressive piece of the so-called "Oxus treasure." Oxus is the ancient name given to the Amu Darya, the river near which was found a treasure including several pieces of jewelry and statuettes which can be attributed to the Achaemenian period.

The bracelet has lost its bright colored stones and its surface is damaged, especially in the dragons' minutely carved wing feathers. In spite of this, its formal value and its perfect execution remain evident.

This work is a typical product of Persian Imperial art, which successfully combines influences from various sources. The Assyrian element is visible in the heavily marked linearity of the relief; the Scytho-Siberian, in the lively energy of the figures of animals; and the Ionic Greek in the stylization, harmony and proportions.

IRANIAN ART OF THE ACHAEMENIAN PERIOD. *Silver Rhyton in the Shape of a Horn.*
The libation vessel in the shape of an animal's horn has been frequently used by different peoples and at different times. This similarity, however, does not imply a historic relationship, as it was due primarily to the actual use of real horns by pastoral populations.

Libation horns with their characteristic animal shapes, usually an ibex or a dragon, were typical products of the Achaemenian metal-working art. It cannot be excluded, therefore, that the Greek *rhyton* in the shape of a deer was influenced by this model.

This work is remarkable for the ridges on the surface of the vase and the sober decoration at the extremities. The dragon figure is in the purest Iranian style, while the decorative design of the palms around the edge shows Greek influence; this motif, however, is also present in Assyrian reliefs.

IRANIAN ART OF THE SASSANIAN PERIOD. *Interior of a Bowl with Bahram V Hunting Lions.*   *p. 68*
The art of the Sassanian period looks to the Achaemenian traditions as the expression of a glorious and almost mythical past. But six centuries of Seleucian and Parthian domination, during which Greek influence had deeply penetrated Iranian culture, could not be forgotten.

It is apparent how much Hellenistic and Roman tradition is present in this

IRANIAN ART
OF THE ACHAEMENIAN PERIOD
Gold bracelet from the "Oxus Treasure"
5th century B.C.
Gold, originally inlaid with enamel or stones;
height 5".
From the Amu Darya basin.

IRANIAN ART
OF THE ACHAEMENIAN PERIOD
Silver rhyton in the shape of a horn
5th century B.C.
Silver, partially covered with gold foil;
height 9 7/8".
From Erzinkan
(Northeast Turkey).

scene representing king Bahram V hunting lions: we see this in the freedom of the naturalistic composition, in the daring perspective and clear spatial structure.

If naturalism is better understood here than in Achaemenian art, however, it is also combined with a more original style, such as the use of a curving line, the source of which is to be found in the traditions of Central Asia.

IRANIAN ART
OF THE SASSANIAN PERIOD
Interior of a bowl, with figure of a king (Bahram V, Gor ?) hunting lions
4th–5th century A.D.
Silver. Previously in the Cunningham Collection.

PERSIA

INDIA

TIBET

CHINA

KASHAN ART. *Plate.*

This is a rare Iranian ceramic piece with white decoration on a cobalt blue background.

The ornamental motif develops from a center divided into four parts composed of ivy leaves set in a radial system; this is repeated in the second circle. The decoration ends at the border with alternately large and narrow branches and leaves symmetrically placed.

It is evident that the plate has been painted directly on the basis of a scheme which is standard in its order and composition.

This kind of plate, with these colors and this curving decoration in a geometrical design, is of historic importance: in all likelihood, the porcelain workshops of the Yüan and Ming Dynasties, beginning in the fourteenth century, were started following the impact of these Persian works.

PERSIAN ART. *Bowl Decorated with Figures of Horsemen.*

A description of the technique used in the manufacturing of this ceramic, which is called "minai," indicates the refinement of its execution. The artist first drew the sketches of the figures with cobalt on a white enamel background. After having been fired once, the figures were painted with various colors; a second firing was necessary to fix the colors.

The figures of knights, birds, sphinxes and trees with crowns of leaves around the branches are drawn in a simple style, as in miniature painting. Sudden movements and the impressionistic character of the scenes are emphasized. The production of this, the richest period of Islamic ceramic art, spread widely in China and Japan.

KASHAN ART
Plate
13th century.
Ceramic with white enamel and green and
black decoration on blue background.

PERSIAN ART
Bowl decorated with figures of horsemen
12th–13th century.
Polychrome enamel ware.

SHIRAZ ART
*Ghenghis Khan addresses the people
in the Mosque of Bukhara*
Ms. Or. 2880, sheet 61/v.
1397–98
Miniature on parchment;
5 3/8″ × 8″.

MOSSUL ART. *Brass Jug.* *p. 71*

In the thirteenth century, under the Seljuk dynasty of the Zinki, Mossul was one of the most important centers for the production of inlaid, decorated metalwork. About twenty of these objects remain, among which is this outstanding example in the British Museum. It differs from similar Persian metalwork of preceding centuries because of its simpler, more solid form. The piece is constructed on an octagonal plan, a form which was already popular in Mesopotamian and Syrian art of the Roman period. Sections of the octagon are decorated within individual zones and four-lobed or circular frames, which are repeated throughout various parts of the vase. The ornamental pattern consists of closely intertwined designs, worked in silver and copper on the brass background. These three colors add to the variety of the vibrating, intense, geometrically conceived surface pattern of the decoration. Such works from northern Mesopotamia, closely related to miniature painting, obtain a similar effect by the disciplined manner in which the various elements of the design are subordinated to an all-over pattern.

SHIRAZ ART. *Ghengis Khan Addresses a Crowd in the Mosque of Bukhara.*

Reproduced here is page 61 *verso* of the *Shansha Name* (Or. 2780), an epic poem of the Mongol people, from the time of Japhet to the successors of Ghengis Khan, down to 1337–38, written for Ilkhan Abu Said by the poet Tabriz Ahmad. The illustration of the manuscript was commissioned in 1397–98 by Ahmad i Galail. Together with the *Anthology* of the poems by Kirmani (British Museum, Add. 18113) it was copied at Baghdad by the famous calligrapher Tabriz Mir Ali and illustrated by the painter Junaid. It is a typical work of the beginning of the arts of painting and calligraphy under the Timurid dynasty. The miniature represents Ghengis Khan who, from a pulpit decorated with geometrical figures, explains to the people in the Mosque of Bukhara that he has been divinely sent as a punishment for their sins.

The picture, with its overlapping figures and flat pulpit, has great surface quality from its use of line and color. Thus the foreground is on the same plane as the background of rocks, flowering and leafy trees and shrubs. It is interesting to note that even the columns of writing above add balance to the composition.

HERAT ART. *Muhammad's Pilgrimage to Heaven.* *p. 74*

Illustrated page of the *Anthology* of Nizami (Or. 6810), sheet 5 *verso*. This *Anthology* was commissioned by the Sultan Mirza Barlas and decorated at Herat in 1494 with 21 miniatures. The fact that in 1564–65 it belonged to the Moghul kings illustrates the relationship between this Gudian painting and its Persian sources. The upper part of the miniature represents Muhammad riding his sacred horse above golden whirling clouds, surrounded by groups of angels. Here a detail of the lower part of the scene is reproduced. Mecca is shown in aerial perspective, in particular the sacred enclosure of the Safa with the Kaaba and its black stone in the center. This representation is especially interesting because it is still close to the late Roman views of the same kind.

SHIRAZ ART. *Iskandar and the Water Nymphs.*

This is a part of the *Anthology* of Jalal Uddin Iskandar (Add. 27261), sheet 286, which contains a selection of poems by Nijami and other poems and studies in astronomy. The manuscript was illuminated by Muhammad al Harvai and Nasir ul Khatib on order of the Sultan Iskandar who called to Shiraz some famous artists from Baghdad. The scene illustrated shows Iskandar (Alexander the Great) who, having crossed the Eastern Sea, reaches a lake on an island: there, with a companion, he watches the water nymphs at play. The composition is beautifully divided by diagonally crossing lines. The moonlit scene is one of the most delicately executed works of poetic fantasy, in which the nymphs, playing, swimming and embracing, or stepping out on the pebbly shore, dressed in leaves, with long hair and wings radiating from their arms, form an unforgettable lyric image.

TURKISH ART. *King Hilar with His Animals.* p. 76

This is a part of *Humayan Name* (Add. 15153), sheet 388. It is one of 165 miniatures adorning that manuscript, a translation into Turkish of the Persian book *Anvar-i-Suhaili,* a collection of Indian tales. The miniature represents King Hilar surrounded by his animals. According to the Brahmins,

HERAT ART
Muhammad's pilgrimage to Heaven
Ms. Or. 6810, sheet 5/v.
1494
Detail.
Miniature on parchment;
5 1/2" × 10 1/2".

SHIRAZ ART
Iskander and the Water Nymphs
Ms. Additional 27261, sheet 286
1410–11
Miniature on parchment;
4" × 6".

he should have killed them, together with his family, in order to purify himself by bathing in their blood. Combined with the conventions of Persian miniature painting we see here reflections of the traditional Art of the Steppes, such as the Black Pen works, with its more linear, simple patterns of line and color. There is also a certain "folk art" quality which contrasts with the more aristocratic style of Persian miniatures.

TURKISH ART
King Hilar with his animals
Ms. Additional 15153, sheet 388.
1589
Detail.
Miniature on parchment;
4 7/8" × 4".

BEHZAD.   *The Caliph Haroun Al Rashid and the Barber,*
from the Nizami Anthology.

The scene belongs to Nizami's *Anthology* (Or. 6810), sheet 27 *verso,* a collection of five poems, based on old legends, either Iranian or of Iranian derivation. It later became a kind of classical model in Moslem literature. The page reproduced here depicts the Caliph Haroun al Rashid in his bath,

BEHZAD
Caliph Haroun al Rashid and the Barber
Ms. Or. 6810, sheet 27/v.
Shiraz 1494.
Miniature on parchment;
5 15/16" × 5 13/16".

دو رخلافت چو بهاروس
راپت عباس کند دون سد
هم شبی پشت بهم خوابکرد
روی باسایش کریاکرد
موی تراشی کوسرش می تیزد
موی بوش نمیر

کای شش آگاه زاستادم
خاص کن امروز مکردیم
خطبه تزوح پراکسن
دخرخود نامزد بندکن
طبع خلیفه قدری کریکشت
باز پذیرین ازرم مکشت
گفت سیاست جکرش تابت
دهشتی ازوحشان یافت
پنخ دیش کرجنس باوری
ورنه کرددی زمن این جت جوی
روزد کردیک نرش ازمود
برد رم قبضه همین ستکه بود

with the barber who proposed to his daughter, and the discovery of the treasure hidden in the barber's house. The miniatures in this wonderful codex are painted by Behzad. We have very few of his original works, though there are many imitations with forged signatures. The painter's career began in 1488–89 with the miniatures of the *Saadi Garden,* now in the Cairo Library, as a pupil of Husain Mirza of the Herat School; he appears here in his full maturity. Having freed himself from the prevailing conventions and formality of the Tabriz and Shiraz Schools, the artist went back to a simpler, fresher and more immediate vision of life. This serenely contemplative world includes lively details, but enfolds everything within a lucid composition which has purity of form as its highest goal; this is obvious here, for example, in the masterful arrangement of the various elements of the background and clear-cut architectural divisions.

SHAM. *King Baber Hunting, from the Autobiography of Baber.*

This is part of the *Baber Name* (Or. 3714), sheet 109 *verso,* a codex with 68 full-page miniatures and 48 small ones with animals and plants. The book is the Persian translation of the Turkish text of the *Autobiography* or journal of Baber, founder of the Moghul Dynasty. This miniature represents Baber watching a hunt on the Hindu-Kush Mountains in the year 1504.

The Moghul School started as a courtly style with a group of Persian painters of the Safavid Dynasty. But ever since the time of the emperor Akhbar, Indian painters were also active in it. In this miniature painted by Sham, one of the most famous artists of his time, the style of many figures points clearly to a Persian origin; but there is something new in the perspective of the scene which moves from the foreground to the middle plane and finally to the far background with its castle. To the purely linear drawing of the surface is added a sculptural modeling in light and shade, particularly in the landscape of rocks, water and trees.

Sham has a distinctive style which can be perceived even in minor details, as well as in the conscious spatial use of the pattern of the flying birds.

GANDHARAN ART. *Relief of King Sibi's Sacrifice to the God Indra.* *p. 80*

This relief represents the offering of Sibi, who cuts up his body piece by piece in order to ransom the dove, according to Indra's request. The god is represented as an eagle. In this scene the king, about to die, is held by the queen, just before the god renounces his demand. It is a characteristic bas-relief of Gandharan art, a projection into northwest India of Hellenism, whose style it inherits and elaborates. At the same time the art of Gandhara establishes an iconography destined to spread extensively, of the life of Sakyamu and of the Buddha and Bodhisattva statues. Our scene is represented at a moment of crisis. Motion and passion, and a pictorial style full of intense light and sudden and lively interaction are all framed within the subtle and graceful rhythms of a classical composition.

INDIAN ART. *Buddha in Meditation.*

Gautama sits meditating under the Bhodi tree, surrounded by the spirit of evil, by the king of air and other figures. He touches the earth and vanquishes every spirit and force. In the composition of this high-relief, which reminds us of the statue at Sarnath, it is still possible to see the mark of a compositional type derived from Hellenistic through Gandharan art. Framed by an arch formed by the two bodies on either side and by the vine-leaves above, the figure of the Buddha is inscribed in a triangular structure. This balanced relationship of elements around a central axis, though not rigorously symmetrical, is remarkably consistent. The axial curves of the figures at the sides emphasize the serene and relaxed rhythmic composition. Even in their minor arts, Indian artists work according to a conscious ideal of harmony; here the sculpture is rendered in a soft shaded way that corresponds to the pattern of curved lines in the relief.

ART OF DANDAN–WILK.   *Bodhisattva* (?).

This painting comes from temple D VII at Dandan-Wilk in Khotan, Central Asia. In contrast to the Miran frescoes, inspired by the style of Gandhara, these paintings obviously relate to Iranian art, like the later Kisil frescoes. It is not certain that the figure represents a Bodhisattva dressed as an Iranian prince; the halo was not restricted to sacred personages, but could be worn by other figures too; for instance, by the donor who commissioned the work. At Bayman, on the other hand, there is a figure of Shiva, also wearing Iranian dress. In this, as in other pictures of this group, the taste for a curving, supple and lively line creates an extraordinarily elegant and lively pattern, full of movement and vitality.

ART OF SOUTHERN INDIA.   *Shiva.*

This sculpture was made by the *cire-perdue,* or lost-wax process, introduced at the time of the Gutpa Dynasty. It is typical of the bronzes produced in Southern India between the ninth and the fourteenth or fifteenth century. It is also among the oldest, as we can see from the torso which is still shaped in a manner reminiscent of the stone statues of Gandhara and Central Indian art. The composition of this statue, with its calculated, balanced rhythm, is animated by a kind of oscillating feeling of suspense that gives life and motion to the figure. Such an effect results from the relationship of the uplifted arms in contrast with the frontal pose, and to the rhythm of the legs which breaks the basic triangular form. This potential movement is emphasized by such decorative elements as the high tiara — with ornament repeated on the arms — the multiple necklace, the serpentine chain over the chest, the belt, the loincloth with animal mask, the flowers interlaced in the locks of hair hanging over both shoulders, the rings on the feet. This decorative opulence draws the viewer's attention in different directions, following, as it were, the vibrations of the statue in the space around it.

ART OF
SOUTHERN INDIA
Shiva
10th century. Bronze.

ART OF TUN–HUANG
Buddha in Prayer
Middle of the 8th century.
Painting on silk.

ART OF TUN–HUANG.   *Buddha in Prayer*.

This T'ang painting was found in 1907 by Stein in the Cave of the Thousand Buddhas. It represents the Buddha praying under the Tree of Enlightenment, seated on lotus flowers on Mount Sumeru, surrounded by four Bodhisattvas and other figures below are the donors who commissioned the painting, one of whom is missing. The painting is executed in several superimposed layers. The parts in relief are marked by sharp lighting, in a technique borrowed from Greek and Roman art. This is true also of the distribution of parts in the composition and of the spatial relations. Other peculiarities of T'ang style show a connection with Indian and Central Asiatic art. In spite of the poor state of preservation, we can appreciate the structure, in which some parts are clearly subordinated to others, resulting in a majestic and imposing whole. This work is particularly important because it reveals the influence of motifs from the Mediterranean on the art of the Far East. Such historical East-West connections became reciprocal in the Middle Ages.

ART OF NORTHERN INDIA.   *The God Canda-Rosana*.

This is the reproduction of sheet No. 166 of the Sanskrit Sutra *Ashta Sasasrika Praina Paramita* (Or. 12461), written with Northern characters and illustrated by sixty-one miniatures contained in squares with figures surrounded by halos of flame. This work belongs to the painting of the Pala Dynasty of Eastern India, of the seventh-eighth centuries whose forms were to continue in Tibetan art. The God Canda-Rosana, who is here an incarnation of Akshobhoya, is an angry and terrifying figure, following a popular iconographical form. In the pattern of revolving scarlet flames, in the exquisite drawing of the lines on the blue body of the god, of his multicolored loincloth with flying ribbons and of the yellow scarves whirling around the body, the artist has created an extraordinarily inspired image by means of a subtle and refined calligraphy.

ART OF NORTHERN
INDIA
The God Canda-Rosana.
Middle of the 10th century.
Miniature on palm leaf;
length 4 7/8".

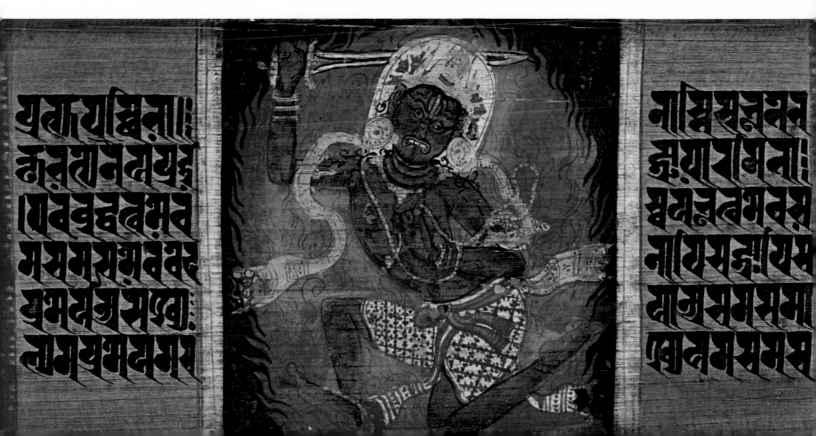

ART OF HONAN. *Head of a Bull.*

This is a wedge-shaped head of a bull, of gilded bronze, with gold and silver whirl-like inlays on the ears. Drilled circles decorate the top of the head, and bands, marked by parallel or oblique stripes, the muzzle and forehead. It probably served as the rudder of a funerary cart, from Lo-yang, in the Honan province, in the period of the Fighting Kingdoms.

CHINESE ART. *Sword Handle.*

We do not know the provenance of this sumptuous piece of jewelry. The decorative whirls remind us again of the art of Honan province in the period of the Fighting Kingdoms, while the motif, as well as the composition of serpents intertwined in a fretwork pattern for this hilt of a ceremonial sword, derive from other rituals in use during the Yin and Chou Dynasties. There is, however, great freedom and independence in the use of the abstract representation and composition. We can recognize the individual forms, repeated in a regular pattern; but at the same time they are lost as they cross each other in an inextricable blend of forms, lines and patterns. Connections with ancient Siberian art cannot be excluded, but the search for a purely objective pattern points to a highly sophisticated, conscious esthetic.

CHINESE ART. *Bear.*

In the Han period, which had a particular taste for bronzework, encouraged by the emperor Wu, the bear symbolized good luck, which is why it was painted on imperial standards. This statue is a compact work in which the sculptural features are reduced to essentials, in a search for monumental effects which was a trend we recognize in other products of the dynasty.

CHINESE ART
Bear
1st century B.C.
Gilt bronze;
Height 7".

ART OF HONAN
Head of a bull
4th century B.C.
Bronze.

CHINESE ART
Sword handle
4th century B.C.
Gold; height 4 3/8".

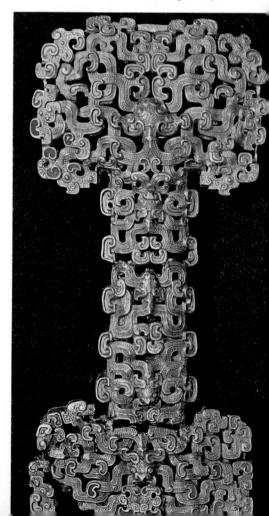

勿謂幽昧　神聽無響
無矜爾榮　天道惡盈
盈無持　爾貴隆:者隆鑒于小星
武彼
隆鑒于小星　武彼
遂此忿　斯則繁爾類

女史司箴敢告庶姬

KU K'AI CHIH. *Instructions of the Governess.*

From the period of the Eastern Tsin (317–386) we have frescoes, drawings on stone and decorated objects; but this painted hand-scroll seems to be the earliest example of a portable painting. Its provenance is complicated. It was originally in the collection of the Ch'ing court; that is why, at the beginning of the scroll, there is a title written by the emperor Ch'ien Lung, with his seals and his sign, a painted orchid. Then the scroll, along with three others by the painter Li Lung-min of the end of the Northern Sung Dynasty, was in the possession of Ku Tsung-i, a famous collector of the late Ming Dynasty. All of these later came into the hands of the Ch'ing court, bearing the mark of Ch'ien Lung, in 1746.

The problem of attribution has been much discussed. For a long time the prevailing opinion was that this scroll was written by the calligrapher Wang I-chih and illustrated by Ku K'ai-chih. The latter was a painter, man of letters and also author of a treatise on painting. Originally from Kiangsu, he was born between 343 and 347, during the dynasty of the Oriental Tsin, and he died around 408. The hypothesis was then advanced that the writing on this scroll could have been done by Emperor Kao-tsung of the Southern Sung, and the illustrations executed by a painter of that time. Finally, some who believe that this scroll is a copy, going back at the latest to the beginning of the T'ang Dynasty, founded their opinion on the statement that this painting belonged to the emperor Huei-tsung (1082–1135) of the Sung Dynasty, who placed his seal on it, and also on the presence of a seal of the T'ang period and on the technique and characters of the calligraphy, which are not later than the T'ang period. The red and black drawing and the shading at the borders point to a time prior to the linear Sung style; they have a close relationship to the painting of the Six Dynasties. The text, about a third of which is missing, according to tradition was compiled by Chang Hua with an imaginary court Governess and refers polemically to the inso-

88

Above and on pages 90–91:
KU K'AI–CHIH
Instructions of the Governess
Ca. 344–408.
Painting on silk.
Four details;
height 9 7/8".

lence and licentiousness of the wife of the emperor Hui-ti of the Tsing Dynasty. The scenes illustrate the text. The text is missing for the first chapter. The third scene, with a hunter's figure, illustrates the idea that everything has its splendor and decadence; the fourth scene, that we must take care of the soul rather than the body; the fifth, that beautiful words are moving even at a distance of a thousand miles, but they are immoral, can create misunderstanding between husband and wife; the seventh scene, that those who grow proud because of a love will eventually lose it; the eighth, that through care and attention one can obtain happiness and through modest consideration one can attain glory. Calligraphic inserts divide the scenes. Traditional Chinese criticism used to compare Ku K'ai-chih's style to a silk thread made by a silkworm in the springtime, signifying, with this comparison, the subtlety, the elastic and continuous development, the delicacy and strength of his work.

The character of the drawing in these *Instructions* is inconceivable after the ink painting of the end of the T'ang period. Even the anthropocentric tendencies, according to which mountains and landscape are smaller than man, is an attitude connecting this work with the style of the period of the Six Dynasties, or before. Considering the extraordinary sensitivity and vitality present in this scroll, we must also exclude the possibility of a later copy; therefore the attribution to Ku K'ai-chih seems validated. This artist, in his writings on art and criticism, affirms he tried to use a line that would be valid for any exterior or inner representation. He joins such a line, in this scroll, to pure colors, particularly red and black, filling in some of the outlined figures, thus alternating colors and lines in a sophisticated rhythm. The master was appreciated, even in later times, for his linear rendering, flexible and exquisite, of undulating clothes, streamers or elaborate hairdos, with subtle accents of scarlet shading and outlining. Even in the T'ang period and later, he was considered to have initiated a great style.

人咸知修其容莫知飾其性性之不飾或愆禮正斧之藻之克念作聖

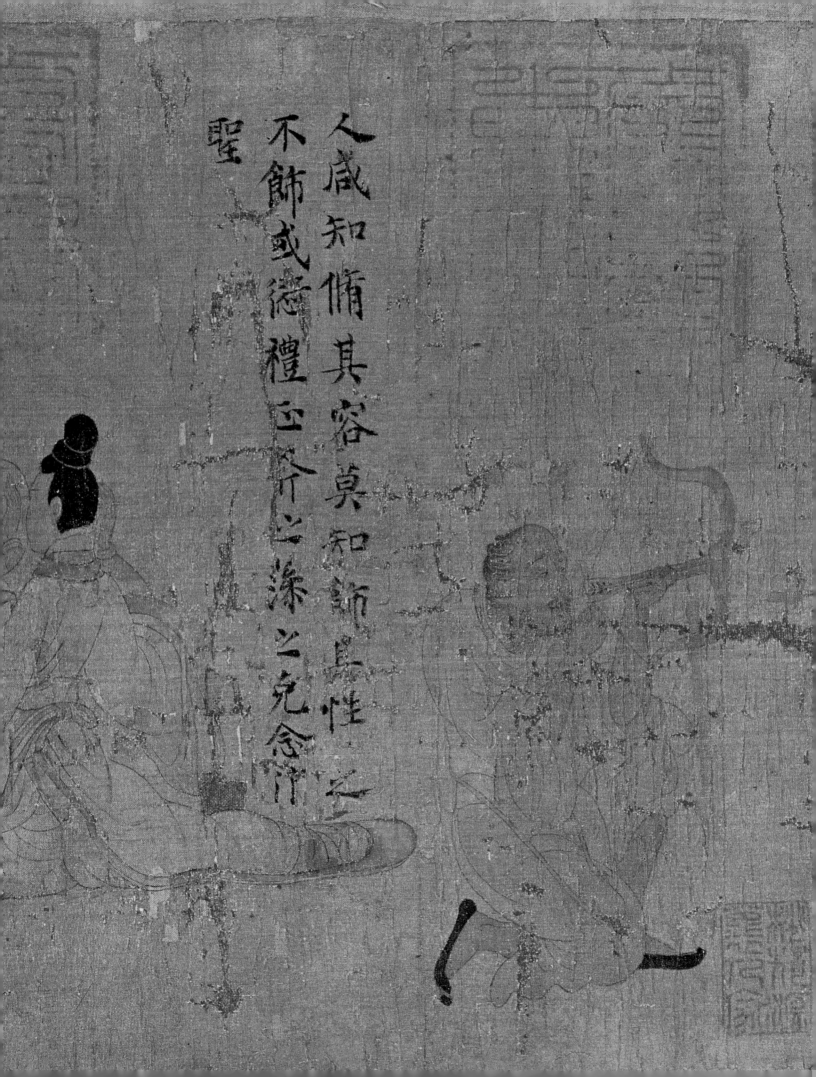

人咸知脩其容莫知飾其性性之
不飾或愆禮正斧之藻之克念作
聖

HOPEH ART. *Statue of an Arhat.*

Quite a few ceramic statues of this kind are found in museums all over the world. It is assumed that they all come from the temples of the Hopeh province, and were produced during the rule of the "barbarian" populations of Liao and Ch'in or perhaps in the Sung period. The green and brown of the garments and the technique used by the artist are those of T'ang three-color ware. The Arhat is seated on a rock in the attitude of meditation. This splendid example expresses, like the others, a total abstraction and aloofness through a triangular composition where curving lines starting from the head are rhythmically echoed. The statue emanates a sense of detachment and isolation in its serene equilibrium.

ART OF HOPEH
Statue of an Arhat
10th–12th century
Glazed pottery;
height 50".

ANCIENT GREECE
ANCIENT ROME

GREEK ART, GEOMETRIC PERIOD.   *Pyxis from Athens.*

The *pyxis,* a boxlike vase, is found in the earliest periods of the Attic ware. In the style of the Geometric Period, known as the Dipylon style, the cover of the *pyxis* has handles in the shape of figures or is decorated with ornamental motifs.

This example belongs to the late Geometric Period, towards the end of the seventh century: the verve of the painted animals seems to predict "Orientalizing" motifs and the Proto-Attic style. The perfect structure of the geometric decoration on a brown background is remarkable, following as it does the elliptical shape of the pot and combining vertical and horizontal elements in striking harmony.

ETRUSCAN ART, IONIAN STYLE.   *Antefix in the Shape of a Girl's Head.*
The antefix in the shape of a girl's head with earrings and leafy crown belongs to a series to be seen in the museums of Berlin, Copenhagen, New

ETRUSCAN ART, IONIAN STYLE
Antefix in the shape of a girl's head
Second half of 6th century B.C.
Painted terra cotta; height 10 5/8".
From Caere (Cerveteri).

GEOMETRIC PERIOD GREEK ART
*Pyxis from Athens with four horses
on the cover*
8th century B.C.
Painted terra cotta; diameter 13".

York, Philadelphia and in the Vatican Museum in Rome. The style of this head, whose color is still well preserved, is close to that of the Attic *Korai* of around 530 B.C. In both Greek and Etruscan works Ionian influence is evident. The surfaces are freely and geometrically decorated, like the Greek examples, but the execution is less refined: some details like the hair, for instance, instead of being carved in relief, are only painted in black.

RUNNING MAN PAINTER. *Amphora with Figure of a Runner.*

The pottery named after Fikellura, near Kameiros in Rhodes, originated around 580 B.C. It was based, at first, on the animal and plant repertory of the earlier Rhodian production. The human figure appears around the middle of the sixth century, while the style imitates the more richly figurative examples of Ionian ware.

The work of the "Running Man Painter," so called because he repeated this motif in several works, contrasts to a certain extent with the more linear and ornamental Corinthian style, a style which influences even Attic black-figure ware and is mainly based on precise and well-defined outlines. We have here, on the contrary, a lively manner, a sort of "expressionism" which is in some ways deforming and humorous, but exceptionally powerful in its use of the free-hand technique; even anatomical details are not incised, but painted in light color on the dark background.

The artist can also transform conventional archaic details, like profile legs and frontal torsos, into more naturalistic positions: the shoulders, for example, are articulated through the movement of the open arms.

While it may be true that this figure of an athlete does not approach the classical Greek ideal, it certainly expresses the concept of speed in an exceptionally effective manner.

AMASIS PAINTER. *Black Figured Olpe.*

Eight vases signed by the potter Amasis still exist. The signatures say *Amasis epoiesen,* which means "Amasis made," or *mepoiesen,* "made me," as in this piece. His name was also found on a fragment from the agora of Athens. It is likely, even if not certain, that Amasis was not only the potter but the painter as well, and executed the decoration, which is stylistically the same on all these vases. There are also many other vases painted by the same hand, without any signature. Scholars have, however, for the sake of convention, named this artist the "Amasis Painter." He was active from around 555 to 525 B.C. and was almost a contemporary of Exekias: he represents therefore the "golden age" of Attic black-figure ware. The *olpe* shown here can be considered one of the greatest achievements of the artist, because of its consistent and noble style. It has a slender shape, with a black handle; the decorated metope is effectively placed on the front, rather than on the side, as in most examples.

ARCHAIC GREEK ART. *Attic "Mastos."*

The *mastoi* (breasts) were footless cups which, once filled, could not be put down before being completely emptied.

The well-balanced scene painted on this *mastos* is composed of four figures, two horsemen fighting in the center and two footsoldiers at the sides. It shows how the influence of the Amasis Painter and of Exekias was felt by lesser artists. Frontality is thoroughly respected: notice the unusual frontal view of the horses, each of which is exactly inscribed in a wedge-shaped space.

ARCHAIC GREEK ART
Attic mastos with figures of footsoldiers and horsemen fighting.
Ca. 530 B.C.
Black-figure pottery;
height 4″; diameter 5″.

ETRUSCAN ART
Lebes (wine jar)
on stand in the form of a tripod.
Ca. 480 B.C.
Bronze, with incised decoration
and attached bronze figures;
height 18".

ETRUSCAN ART. *Lebes on Stand in the Form of a Tripod.*
There are several funeral urns of this shape from Capua, typical of the
Etrusco-Campanian area. Remarkable is the motif of the four horsemen in
a circle, apparently flying diagonally off into space, as if they were pushed in
opposite directions by a centrifugal force. Two of the horsemen, with crests
in the shape of swans, are represented in the act of shooting the enemy. The
spring of the horses and the carefully alternated gestures of the horsemen
create a rhythm of dynamic, changing relations.

MEIDIAS PAINTER.   *Red Figured Hydria.*

This *hydria,* or water jar, is signed by the potter Meidias. The "Meidias Painter," who may be the same person, operated around the last twenty years of the fifth century B.C. He is representative of a period in which the vase painters still refused to use perspective and tonal shades, by this time commonly used in large-scale painting. On this *hydria,* however, the artist achieves some special effects in the composition of the scene, for example, where the figures are placed on different levels in a perspective view. He also uses lines to obtain coloristic effects of light and shade.

GREEK ART.   *Mirror Cover with the Story of Phaedra.*

Phaedra declares to an attendant her love for Hippolytos, while Eros, hovering behind her, grabs her hair with his right hand to attest his power. This scene, which reminds us of Phaedra as she is described in Euripides, certainly has something theatrical about it. The condition of the bronze makes it difficult to appreciate the total effect of the piece, which was probably remarkable, as some details still show. Among the finest are Phaedra's tresses and the folds covering her left ankle, which in their dramatic effects can be compared to the art of Pheidias' school.

GREEK ART
Aphrodite and Pan Playing Knucklebones.
3rd century B.C.
Decoration on the reverse
of a mirror cover.
Incised bronze; diameter 7 1/4".
From Corinth (?).

GREEK ART.   *Aphrodite and Pan Playing Knucklebones.*

This is a rare example reflecting the effect of Etruscan "major" art in contrast to the large mass production of Etruscan incised mirrors. The artist has a great talent for drawing and mastering perspective, and he creates a sort of dialogue between the figures in the scene by means of lively gestures and mimicry. The subject anticipates the "idyllic" and allegoric themes of some Pompeian painting, such as *Pan and Eros Quarreling* and *The Merchant of Erotes.*

GREEK ART (Corinthian work)
Back of a mirror with a maenad.
End of 5th century B.C.
Incised bronze,
figure in silver;
diameter 6 7/8".

GREEK ART.   *Back of a Mirror with a Maenad.*

This mirror back has a drawing which has been deeply incised and covered with silver. It is a product of a graphic art; and indeed the effect is similar to that of contemporaneous vase painting. The difficulty of fixing the design on metal could explain the quality of the line, which is less precise and thus perhaps more attractive to modern taste. It is likely, however, that this effect is due to the condition of the metal, particularly to the loss of some of the silver along the edges.

PHEIDIAS AND ASSISTANT.   *Dione and Aphrodite.*   pp. 104–105

The east pediment of the Parthenon, which represented Athena's birth, was conceived and executed earlier than the western one, representing the contest between Athena and Poseidon for the soil of Attica. The central group of the east pediment had been removed before the 1687 explosion; in fact

On pages 104–105:
GREEK ART
PHEIDIAS AND ASSISTANT
Dione and Aphrodite.
Ca. 435 B.C.
Pentelic marble; height 43".
From the east pediment
of the Parthenon, Athens.

the drawings of 1674 show only the side groups of gods and goddesses who were present at the contest. The two goddesses at the right end of the pediment have been identified as Aphrodite reclining on her mother's lap. This group can be considered to come closest to the pictorial style which is realized in the western pediment. The folds have been treated with exceptional freedom and the "wet" drapery molds the contour of the bodies with naturalistic effects.

WORKSHOP OF PHEIDIAS. *Centaur and Lapith Fighting.*

The "Elgin Marbles," removed and collected by Lord Elgin from 1799 to 1801, have been in the British Museum since 1816. These pieces represent a large portion of the sculptures which decorated the Parthenon. The collection includes 15 metopes from the south side, the only ones not defaced by the Christians because of their less noticeable position; 56 relief slabs of the continuous frieze, about 50 feet long, sculptured around the cell wall and partially destroyed by the 1687 explosion; and 12 sculptures from both pediments. This collection gathers, therefore, whatever remains of the original decoration, with the exception of the group of Cecrops and Pandrosos, still in place on the western pediment of the temple. The metopes were executed at an earlier stage: in 442–441 B.C. the columns were fluted, and we assume, therefore, that the ceiling had been already completed to the top. The pediments were executed from 438 to 432 B.C.; work on the frieze probably was carried out in the period in between, but continued over a long enough time to influence the sculptures of the pediments.

The tradition according to which the decoration of the Parthenon is due to Pheidias is generally accepted by modern scholars. As Plutarch writes, "Pheidias supervised everything"; which apparently means that though he did not personally execute the works — with few exceptions, such as the carving of some details of special significance, or some finishing touches — he conceived, projected and directed the work. Modern scholars, however, believe that Pheidias not only made a general plan of the works and directed their execution, but actually prepared models in all details and educated the craftsmen to what may be called the "Parthenon style." This style had been elaborated by the artist during fifteen years of activity. We can well conclude that to Pheidias, and Pheidias alone, this enormous enterprise should be credited, in spite of the presence of many different workshops and personalities who added their own contribution. Perfect collaboration between artist and helpers is not yet fully accomplished in the metopes, which were completed at an earlier stage. The craftsmen's manners are therefore still evident, even though they are based on Pheidias' models. The 30th metope of the southern side, representing the fight between Centaurs and Lapiths, for instance, as well as the fourth on the same side, were sculptured by craftsmen still influenced by the severe style of Myron. This Myronian school seems also to have influenced the sharp modeling and incisive details of the anatomy; the rigidity of the torsion in the Lapith's hips, for example, reminds us somewhat of Myron's *Diskobolos.*

GREEK ART
WORKSHOP OF PHEIDIAS
Centaur and Lapith Fighting.
447–442 B.C.
30th metope of the south side
of the Parthenon in Athens.
Pentelic marble;
50″ × 52 3/4″.

PHEIDIAS AND COLLABORATOR. *The Ilissos or Cephisos River.*
The statue, which probably represents the Cephisos or Ilissos River, was placed on the left corner of the western pediment, in the same position as the Dionysos of the east pediment. This statue clearly represents the last phase of Pheidias' style in the Parthenon. In the contest between Centaurs and Lapiths, the Lapith still shows traces of the primitive frontality; and Dionysos is actually the earliest statue to be placed in a three-dimensional space in a natural position, so that he can be understood from any point of view. Any further achievements would have been inconceivable without this fundamental change. Dionysos, however, when placed on the pediment could not be conveniently appreciated from below. Therefore the Cephisos was probably made after the intermediate phase of Dione and Aphrodite, in an even more naturalistic position. Though it has smaller proportions, the Cephisos is placed in a three-dimensional space, like Dionysos, and it is more naturalistically modeled, especially in the details of muscles. It is conceived to be seen from the front. In European sculpture similar effects are found in Michelangelo's *Pietà* in St. Peter's or Bernini's *St. Theresa*.

GREEK ART
PHEIDIAS AND ASSISTANT
The Ilissos or Cephisos River
Ca. 435–432 B.C.
Pentelic marble;
height 33".
From the west pediment
of the Parthenon in Athens.

PHEIDIAS AND COLLABORATOR. *Iris.*

The torso of the statue of Iris, which was located behind Poseidon's chariot, shows the use of the convention of clinging or "wet" folds, in accordance with the vibrant, dynamic rhythm which prevails in the sculpture of the western pediment.

GREEK ART. *Head of Hypnos.*

Hypnos, god of Sleep and brother of Death, is represented in a thoughtful expression, with wings attached to each temple, mouth partly opened and drowsy eyes.

A well-preserved statue in the Prado Museum represents the god pouring his magic fluid over mortals.

GREEK ART. *Demeter from Cnidos.*

This statue of Demeter was discovered in 1812 in the sacred area of Demeter and Kore in Cnidos, and unearthed only in 1858. This is an outstanding example of the statuary of the second half of the fourth century B.C. The neck and the head, expressly made by the sculptor to be detachable, were found separately and are less damaged than the rest of the body. The contrast between the smooth flesh and the sharp edges of the drapery is therefore more emphasized than was originally intended. The weathering of the stone, moreover, has further shortened the upper part of the statue: it had already been foreshortened, as it was planned to be seen from below. The loss of the arms and the sides of the throne, as also the badly damaged

GREEK ART
(or Roman copy from Greek original)
Head of Hypnos (Sleep)
4th century B.C.
Bronze: height 8".
From Perugia.

GREEK ART
Demeter from Cnidos
Ca. 340–330 B.C.
Parian marble; height 60 1/4".
From Cnidos.

knees, make our appreciation of the statue more difficult. The well-preserved parts of the figure, however, and particularly the mass of heavy and naturalistic folds on her breast, give the measure of the excellence of the artist. He reminds us of the late period of Pheidias' art, rather than the mannerism of his followers, in his ability to sublimate even the conventional motif of a draped female figure.

HELLENISTIC ART. *Two Women Talking.*
The earliest terra cottas of the Classical and Hellenistic periods are named after Tanagra, a city in Boeotia which first achieved excellence in this field. Similar works originated, however, from various other locations. In the Hellenistic period, Smyrna and Myrina in Asia Minor, and Taranto in Italy were well known for their terra cottas. Most of the "Tanagras" found in good condition come from tombs in which were placed amulets, idols or statuettes of attendants according to ancient custom. After the fourth century B.C. figures of gods became rare and statuettes of ladies in fashionable dresses or scenes of everyday life became increasingly frequent.

This private conversation between two women shows a delicate style and is carefully composed in a pyramidal structure. All the works of this period have a lively and spontaneous expression and show an interest in the woman's world, which apparently had not drawn much attention before. The same feature will be found, many centuries later, in the porcelains of the eighteenth century.

GREEK ART OF THE HELLENISTIC PERIOD. *Head of Aphrodite.*
The left hand of the statue to which this head belonged is known; it holds a

112

GREEK ART OF THE
HELLENISTIC PERIOD
Head of Aphrodite
2nd–1st century B.C.
Bronze; height 15″.
(the full-length statue was
probably more than 7 feet long).
From Satala in Armenia.
Formerly in The Castellani Collection;
purchased by the British Museum in 1873.

HELLENISTIC ART
Two women talking
3rd century B.C.
Painted terra cotta; height 7 1/4″.
From Myrina (Asia Minor).

GREEK ART OF THE HELLENISTIC
PERIOD
Aphrodite
Ca. 200 B.C.
Bronze; height 21 1/2″.
Found near Patras.

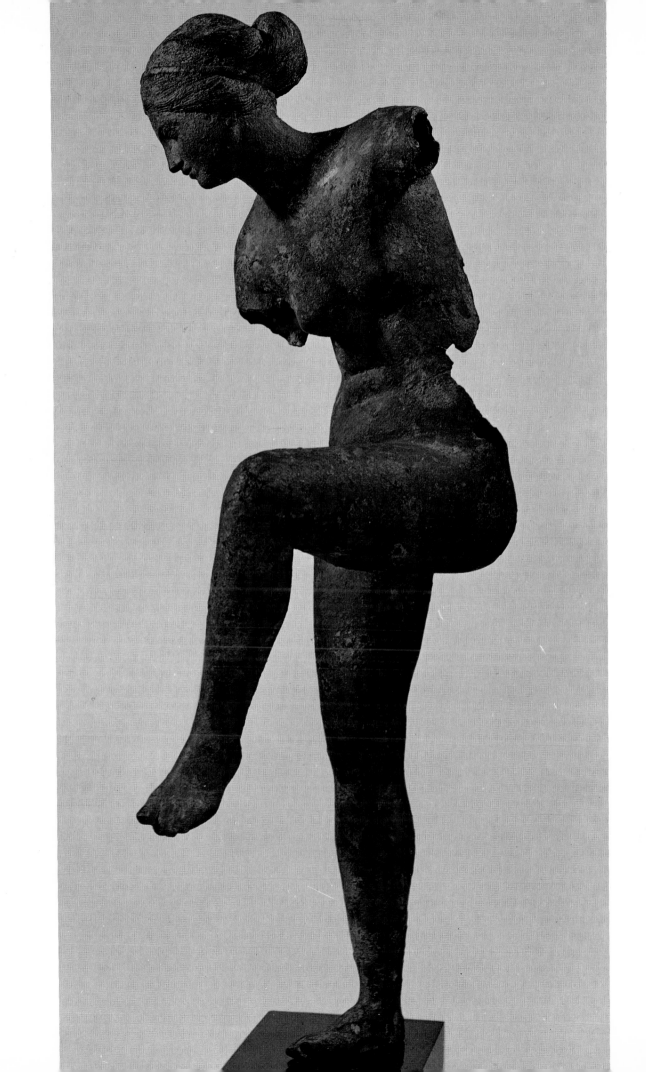

border of a garment. The artist therefore was probably imitating a model of an Aphrodite of the fourth century B.C. This head is an abstract creation, even though it has an apparent naturalism: the artist's purpose was to represent an ideal of beauty, rather than the features of an individual woman. The shape of the face is perfectly oval; eyes, nose and mouth are balanced; the stylized, clearly incised hair seems to be waved in a natural way, though it actually follows an arbitrary serpentine rhythm. Two curls on the goddess' forehead give an idea of this accurate, manneristic style, as well as of its excellent technical quality. It reminds us of a goldsmith's technique, as in Cellini's work, or in the sculptures of the Fontainebleau studios.

On page 116:
ROMAN ART
Helmet with mask-like visor
1st–2nd century A.D.
Embossed and incised bronze;
height 10 1/2".
Found in 1786 at Ribchester
(Bremetennacum Veteranorum)
in Lancashire.
Formerly in the Townley Collection.

ROMAN ART
Head of the Emperor Hadrian
Bronze; height 16".
Found around the middle of last century
in the Thames under London Bridge.
A right hand, found later
not far from the Bridge,
might also belong to this colossal statue.

GREEK ART OF THE HELLENISTIC PERIOD. *Aphrodite.*   *p. 113*
This rather damaged statuette represents a nude Aphrodite of rare elegance. A comparison with a bronze statuette in the Louvre, which is similar to this one, though rougher, allows us to reconstruct the goddess' pose. She stands, without any support, as she fastens or unfastens a sandal, either before or after the bath, while her left hand gropes in the air to maintain her balance.

ROMAN ART. *Head of the Emperor Hadrian.*
The bronze head here shown is probably a portrait of the emperor Hadrian. Compared to the severe and imposing official portraits of the Hellenistic period, however, this provincial statue reflects a marginal style still linked to Republican traditions: this is shown by the simplicity as well as the vitality of the features. This regional style flourished in official portraiture as late as the third century.

HELLENISTIC ROMAN ART
Head of Augustus
27 B.C.–14 A.D.
Bronze; height 18 3/4".
Found in the excavations at Meroe
in the Sudan, 1910.

HELLENISTIC ROMAN ART. *Head of Augustus.*
This superb *Head of Augustus,* once part of a full-length statue, is obviously the product of an Alexandrian workshop. In comparison to heroic portraits of Alexander the Great, it reveals considerable individualization of Octavian, the man, while adhering to the Roman tradition, and to the iconography of Augustus. If, however, this iconography originated in Alexandria itself, this head from Meroe could well be close to the archetypical example.

ROMAN ART. *Helmet with Mask-Like Visor.*   *p. 116*
This display helmet is made up of two thin pieces of metal, originally joined by a strap or a hinge. The anthropomorphic mask is encircled by a turreted frieze, like Roman honorary crowns, and surmounted by figures of Cupids. The main decoration shows horsemen and soldiers in action. Helmets of this shape have been found in Bulgaria, Germany and in Great Britain. They are also mentioned by the historian Arrian. A similar example, with a silver-plated mask and iron skull cap — possibly for use in battle — was found at Homs in Syria and is now in the Damascus Museum.

METALS
IVORIES
TEXTILES
ENAMELS
CERAMICS

EARLY CHRISTIAN ROMAN ART. *Wedding Casket of Projecta.*

The *Casket of Projecta* was found in 1793 in Rome near the church of S. Silvestro and S. Martino on the Esquiline. It was together with various other precious objects and can be ascribed to the time of the emperor Theodosius or Honorius. Although the people to whom it was given were undoubtedly Christian, the piece shows a peculiar persistence of pagan motifs. The inscription reads, *"Secunde et Projecta vivatis in Christo"* [Secundus and Projecta, may you live in Christ]. The chest is in the shape of a double truncated pyramid with a rectangular base. Four scenes are represented on the four sloping sides of the cover: on the front side, Venus in a shell; on the back side, the bride led to the wedding; and on the two smaller sides, Nereids and sea monsters. Reproduced above is one of the smaller sides with the figure of a Nereid and a sea monster, Eros and dolphins. A glimpse of the front and the back sides can be seen at the right and the left. Although the subjects are traditional, this work does not follow classical schemes of ideal perfection: here, as in contemporaneous ivory diptychs and textiles, the technique used allows particular effects of color and a vigorous execution. The artist freely, sometimes whimsically, selected the parts to be cov-

118

EARLY CHRISTIAN
ROMAN ART
Wedding casket of Projecta
Ca. 380 A.D.
Embossed (*repoussé*) and partially
gilded silver;
21 3/4″ × 11″.
From the Esquiline, Rome.

LATE ROMAN ART
(BY THE SILVERSMITH EUTHERIOS?)
Plate with satyr and maenad
4th century A.D.
Silver; diameter 7 3/8".
Found together with several pieces
at Mildenhall (Suffolk) in 1942.

ered with gold, without following any established pattern. So every second ridge of Venus' shell is gilded, for example, while the olive leaves on the trapezoidal frames are gilded in groups of three or four or five.   (*D.G.*)

EUTHERIOS.   *Plate with Satyr and Maenad.*

This silver plate representing a satyr and a maenad dancing together probably is one of a series. A similar piece with Pan and a maenad playing music was found in Mildenhall and is today also in the British Museum. Both plates have inscribed on the back the name of the silversmith or owner, in Greek letters in the genitive case: "*Eutheriou.*" The style, with its classicizing tendency, seems to be that of the Roman aristocracy. The imitation of classic motifs is accurate; it is not difficult, however, for an expert to recognize in this piece the typical features of the late fourth century. The well defined outlines do not have the purpose of modeling, but rather of pictori-   119

ally interpreting the forms. The decoration is free and graceful, and the execution technically excellent.

It is understandable that this kind of work, kept in the "treasuries" of courts and cathedrals, had such a great importance for the craftsmen of the Carolingian period. (D.G.)

EARLY CHRISTIAN ROMAN BYZANTINE ART. *Archangel.*

This large ivory plaque, which had probably been in Canterbury since the fourteenth century, is an outstanding example of the rich early Christian and Byzantine ivory production. It is usually dated between the fifth and sixth century, though some scholars have tentatively suggested the eighth. The most probable date is, however, the fifth century: the features of the face, the attitude of the figure, the setting in a frame, are similar to those of the consular diptychs and of several works of art of that century, such as the *Angels* of the mosaics at Ravenna. The minute folds, the detailed and pointed architectural decoration are less common, though not inconsistent with that style. Notice the classic correctness of this figure, solemnly placed under an arch. The artist, however, does not appear to be concerned with a plausibly spatial setting for the figure. While the Archangel's feet, for instance, are represented as though seen from the spectator's eye level, the steps on which they tread are seen in perspective from a lower level. (D.G.)

ART OF THE EASTERN MEDITERRANEAN. *Decorated Textile.*

Such decorated textiles, either Byzantine or Coptic or early Islamic, have their origins in the Hellenistic Roman and Late Roman tapestry. Important elements from Sassanian-Persian art, however, mostly ornamental and schematic and connected with Far Eastern cultures, were soon added to Hellenistic naturalism: the motif of the two facing horsemen is probably Sassanian. The decoration of this fragment of a textile is further stylized within the strictly perpendicular pattern of the lines of the weft and the warp of the cloth. The artist's imagination has made the most of the limitations of his material: he has shown diagonal and curved lines, for example, by means of a geometric "step pattern." This extreme stylization shows we are already beyond the limits of Roman art and entering the Middle Ages. (D.G.)

EARLY CHRISTIAN
ROMAN BYZANTINE ART
Ivory panel with Archangel
Ca. 5th century A.D.
Originally part of a diptych;
height 16 3/4".

ART OF THE EASTERN
MEDITERRANEAN
*Fragment of a decorated textile
with figures of horsemen and animals
sewn as an "appliqué"
on the remains of a linen garment.*
7th–8th century A.D.
Silk; height 18".
Gift of Rev. W. Mac Gregor (1886);
said to come from Egypt.

LATE CELTIC ART
Display shield
1st century B.C.
Gilded bronze with enamel;
height 32".
Found in the bed of the Thames River
near Battersea.

LATE CELTIC ART. *Display Shield.*

In this object, we see how the typical Late Celtic goldsmith's art reached a neo-classical, sophisticated purity. The shield itself is shaped in a complex geometrical figure. Three ornamental disks are connected by metal buttons along the vertical axis; these disks are decorated by embossed curving lines, which are beautifully stylized. Small metal plaques, on which a swastika is marked, are placed in the volutes. It is not easy to describe so abstract an art; it is enough to notice that a delicate, almost musical decorative alternation flows into the symmetrical structure of the whole. Many similar objects have been found in river beds, mostly in good condition. The position of the handle on the back of the shield, as well as the delicate, fragile decoration of the front, has lead scholars to believe that it was used for display, as an offering or "ex-voto" to the gods of rivers.

LATE CELTIC ART. *Mirror Back.*

The decoration of the back of this mirror is extremely elegant, composed of spirals and curving lines which were engraved by burin on the surface, with crosshatch motifs. This mirror is one of the finest examples of the Celtic metalwork technique, together with a similar example in the Gloucester Museum. The spirals are evidently stylized aquatic motifs and seem to give to the surface a full range of shades and reflections. Mirrors in ancient times were made by polishing a metal or ivory surface: their nature was therefore illusory and imaginative, just as the images they reflected were vague and unreal.

SAXON ART. *Lock for a Purse.* p. 124

Sutton Hoo is an archeological district famous for the eleven tombs found there. It is located on a sand hill at Woodbridge in eastern England, not far from the mouth of the Deben River. The place had long been the object of occasional excavations, but only in 1939 was an important discovery made by professionals who unearthed a ship almost 25 meters long. This ship was conceived as symbolic transportation to the life beyond. Inside it several objects were stored, to be taken by the dead on his long trip, including weapons, coins, clothing and pieces of furniture. No traces of corpses were found, which leads us to believe that in all likelihood the ship was a memorial rather than a tomb. We may deduce from the rich equipment that it was made for a very important personage, such as a king or a ruler of eastern England: probably Aethelhere, who died in 655 A.D. This date would coincide with the age of the coins.

The buckle illustrated here, originally used as a lock for a purse, is one of the objects found in the "tomb." Its metallic parts were originally fitted on a bone or ivory background; it is now shown on a white piece of wood. Thin, braided golden strings mark the outside of the buckle; inside there are various ornamental motifs, both with and without figures. On both sides is represented the Oriental theme of a man assaulted by two wild pigs, while in the

LATE CELTIC ART
Display shield
1st century B.C.
Gilded bronze with enamel;
height 32".
Found in the bed of the Thames River
near Battersea.

LATE CELTIC ART
Mirror back
End of 1st century B.C.
Incised and patinated bronze,
with handle of linked, soldered iron rings;
height 13 3/4".
From Desborough, Northants.

123

center are symmetrical groups showing two birds of prey seizing two ducks. Both these subjects evidently refer to the power of the monarch. The upper decorations are symmetrical and wholly stylized, and well known by the German tribes who had imitated them from Oriental art.

The jewelry from Sutton Hoo is close stylistically to the products of the Kent workshops of the Jutes, where a Merovingian influence is to be noted.

SAXON ART
Lock for a purse
First half of 7th century.
Gold, garnets, glass and enamel;
Length 7 1/2".
Found at Sutton Hoo,
Suffolk (England).

CAROLINGIAN ART. *Crystal of Lothair II.*

The narrative decoration on this rock-crystal disk is developed clockwise. It starts from the upper scene: Susanna, bathing in her pool, with perfumes and vases around her, is faced by two elders. Behind them two servants are running to help. The group on the right represents Joachim's house, where the elders are plotting to kidnap Susanna. On a lower level the elders are condemning and leading her to death; but Daniel comes to her rescue and proves the two men guilty; they are subsequently stoned. In the center are Susanna and Daniel with servingmen.

The art of engraving gems, which flourished during the Roman period, was revived by Carolingian artists. In this object, the late Roman tradition is evident in the accurate execution of the figures, as well as in their free, realistic gestures. The influence of a new taste, however, stylistically close to the miniatures of the *Psalter of Utrecht* and to the contemporaneous workshops of Reims, is also felt.

The history of this object deserves to be briefly summarized. Around the first half of the tenth century it was owned by the wife of Eilbert, Count of

CAROLINGIAN ART
Crystal of Lothair II
Gold frame of the 15th century.
Engraved rock-crystal.
In the center is the
following inscription:
"Lothair king of the Franks ordered [it]
to be made." This is Lothair II
who ruled 855–859. It depicts the
Story of Susanna and the Elders
from the Bible,
Book of Daniel, chapter XII.

Florennes. The latter gave it to the Bishop of Reims as a pledge for a valuable horse; but when the Bishop refused to give it back, the Count besieged and set fire to the Cathedral where the Bishop took refuge. The prelate ran out with the crystal hidden under his clothes and surrendered to the Count. Later the Count repented for the sacrilege, and donated the piece to a monastery he founded at Waulsort. The crystal was kept there until the French Revolution. Around the middle of the nineteenth century a Belgian antique dealer, who said he had found it in the Meuse River, sold the crystal in France for twelve francs. It was subsequently owned by the English collector Bernal, at the auction of whose collection in 1855, at Christie's, it was purchased by the British Museum.

ITALIAN BYZANTINE ART. *The Resurrection of Lazarus.*

Christ entering Bethany, followed by an apostle, meets Martha and Mary. Behind them the mummy of Lazarus is standing in its coffin. The solemn gestures and looks, the attitude of the figures and the noble landscape of the city give a large, almost monumental proportion to this small plaque.

Macedonian influences are to be noted in this work, along with the stylized art of the Ottonian period.

ROMANESQUE ART. *Oliphant.*

Called "oliphants" (from the Latin *elephantus*), these objects are more commonly known as "horns" and were sounded for hunting or war. Two silver strips protect the hollow ivory from splitting, or else served to attach a shoulder-belt. The tusk is decorated by carved twisting relief lines forming circles; within these are inscribed mythological monsters. The Mozarabic origin of these themes, as well as the type of object, indicate that this work is a product of Islamic influence. Some details of style seem to point to an Italian origin, probably from the region of Lombardy. It is safer, however, to state that it bears some similarity to objects with relief decorations used in Lombardy during the Romanesque period. Spain was the native country of these objects, the most famous of which is the "oliphant" of Roland, Charlemagne's paladin, originally kept in the Cathedral of St. Sernin of Toulouse and presently to be seen in the Dupuy Museum.

ITALIAN BYZANTINE ART
The Resurrection of Lazarus
Between the 11th and 12th century.
Ivory; height 7 1/2".
Wing of a diptych. Traces of ancient
restorations on the vertical breaks.
Gift of Pius II to the church of
S. Andrea of Amalfi. In the 18th century it
was still in the convent of the
Holy Apostles (SS. Apostoli), Naples.

ROMANESQUE ART
Oliphant
11th century.
Ivory;
length 21".
Northern Italy.

GODEFROID DE HUY
Copper Cross
Middle of the 12th century.
Decorated with enamel (*champlevé*)
and precious stones;
height 14 1/2".

GODEFROID DE HUY. *Copper Cross.*

In the center of the cross and at the ends of each of the arms are five small pictures depicting various scenes from the Old Testament. The cross is set with semi-precious stones and the pictures are done in polychrome enamel. Each scene is titled. The center one shows Jacob as he places his hands upon his adopted sons, Manasseh and Ephraim; they kneel at his sides as he blesses them (*Genesis,* 68). At the top of the cross are Moses and Aaron with the brazen snake (*Numbers,* 21). At the bottom of the cross Joshua and Caleb carry an enormous cluster of grapes on their shoulders (*Numbers,* 13). On the left, the widow of Salepta carries a cross to Elijah. On the right, an Israelite paints the letter T (tau) with the blood of a slaughtered lamb on the door of his house (*Exodus,* 12). Jacob's crossed arms symbolize that all these stories are motifs from the Old Testament which refer, as analogies, to the New Testament. Each scene is a prototype of Jesus' sacrifice on the cross. A similar cross, perhaps by the same artist, is found in the Victoria & Albert Museum, London.

The *champlevé* technique spread into the valleys of the Rhine, the Meuse and the Lorraine and had Limoges as its chief center. Godefroid de Huy belonged to this school of Limoges, which was later to produce the famous Nicolas de Verdun. The style, which combines a taste for luxurious ornamentation with a mystic symbolism, obviously shows the influence of Suger, the great patron and abbot of St. Denis.

MOSAN ART
Henry of Blois and Angels
England (?) ca. 1150.
Enameled copper (*champlevé*);
diameter 7".

MOSAN ART. *Henry of Blois and Angels.*

The work is formed by two semicircular plates of copper, engraved and painted with enamels in the depressions, according to the *champlevé* tech-

nique in which Godefroid de Huy excelled. This work has indeed been attributed to him; he could have executed it on a trip to England.

The horizontal inscription refers to a Bishop Henry, to be identified with Henry of Blois, Bishop of Winchester. Other inscriptions run along the two lines that enclose the circle. The outer one praises Henry, whose intelligence is said to be greater than the Muses's, his eloquence greater than Cicero's. The other circle contains a prayer that the donor will be sent to Heaven, but as late as possible, because all of England hopes that the man who keeps England in peace will go on living. The Latin inscription is to be attributed to Henry himself. The present piece is one of several fragments dispersed in private English and French collections. All together, these fragments made up some kind of panel. This is probably what the bishop is represented as holding in his arms, along with his pastoral staff. He is prostrating himself, as a donor making an offering.

This was obviously part of an altar-front or a reliquary, given by Henry, it seems, for the shrine of St. Swithun in Winchester Cathedral.

RHENISH ART. *Reliquary in the Shape of a Head.*

The composite technique of this type of work is quite different from real sculpture. The head is not, in fact, sculptured in the round. Instead, the mass is externally defined; it is formed by means of planes, which are conceived of as a series of curved raised surfaces attached to the wooden core as an *appliqué*. The style is still essentially Romanesque, but the exquisite rendering of the hair is reminiscent of the classical style, and can be compared to that of the earliest of the recumbent tomb figures of St. Denis. Reliquaries were made in many different shapes. In the Byzantine era, for example, they were invariably in the form of small sarcophagi. In the Middle Ages, in the West, they were made in anthropomorphic forms corresponding to the relics of the saints which were put inside the containers: arms, torsos or heads, as in the present case. Later, the forms of reliquaries as well as that of other kinds of votive offerings evolved according to the major style of the period.

RHENISH ART
Reliquary in the shape of a head
Early 12th century.
Embossed, incised silver,
attached to a wooden core,
height 13 3/8".
Figures of the 12 Apostles
at the base of the reliquary
are embossed (*repoussé*) and incised silver.
From the Cathedral of Basilea (?);
the identity of the saint is unknown.

ENGLISH ART. *Round Brooch.*   *p. 132*

This convex silver brooch is divided by a circular molding into two concentric circles. Within the center circle are five human figures. The one in the middle holds in his hands two horns, with four plants jutting out of each. Around this central figure are four figures in almond-shaped spaces. By their typical poses, these characters seem to represent the senses.

In the outside ring are human, animal and abstract figures in smaller circles. The division of the brooch into these four almond-shaped sections — obtained with a compass — may indicate the four quarters of the world, but the cosmic significance of the symbols and their relationships is not completely clear. The outlines are emphasized by means of the black enamel — *nigellum* — used to fill in the spaces between the figures. The brooch is probably a product of provincial folk art.

ENGLISH ART. *Painted Tiles.*

This is a typical workshop product of the Middle Ages, around the fourteenth century. These tiles are characteristic of a well known procedure used as a substitute for painting or mosaic. The technique is linear, and the style is reminiscent of contemporary miniature painting. The figures are incised with a nail and painted yellow on a red background. The scenes shown, which must have been part of a great altar, illustrate rare and delightful anecdotes from the *Apocrypha*. The drawing is spontaneous and very free. The style is akin to that of wood engraving, which came into use soon after this time; yet the technique is different. The illustrations themselves are typical of those of the printed *Biblia Pauperum*, with its comic-strip-like characters.

ENGLISH ART
Painted tiles
Early 14th century.
Ceramic; each 5 1/4″ wide.
Originally from the walls of a chapel
in the Cambridge region.

ENGLISH ART
Round brooch
9th century.
Silver and enamel;
diameter 4 1/8″.

ENGLISH ART.   *The Kiss of Judas.*

This is a remarkable example of the preservation of an iconographic motif made famous in Italy by Giotto. Not only the central group, but all of the spectators, Peter, Mark and the assassins are also drawn up in a semi-circle under the curve of the Gothic arch within an intricate framework, indicating a highly sophisticated technique.

Opus Anglicanum, as English embroidery was called in Europe, met with great success on the Continent. It contributed to the formation of various local cultures because of the concentrated stylistic ideas which it brought in its wake. Its center of diffusion seems to have been London.

FLEMISH ART
Decorated shield
15th century.
Gilded wood and tempera;
height 32″.

FLEMISH ART. *Decorated Shield in Gilded Wood and Tempera.* *p. 135*
This splendid example of a courtly tournament shield, with a socket for the lance, is divided into two panels, like a diptych. It represents a love scene. To the left stands an elegant lady; to the right, a warrior on bended knee with his head uncovered is being presented by a skeleton. In the ornamental scroll is inscribed his motto: "You or death." It was probably commissioned for a special event, since the faces of the characters, especially the one of the knight, seem to be portraits.

FLEMISH ART. *Pyx.*
This is probably a composite work. The base and the floral wreath that encircles the cover and the handle are in incised metal. The boy at the top holding the shield, on which is a blazon, seems to be from another hand. Yet the parts blend together into a harmonious whole. The cup is illustrated with charming stories reminiscent of similar manuscript illustrations. These are executed in the *niello* technique — filling in engraved silver with a black sulphur compound.

GERMAN ART. *Decorated Silver Cup.*
The decoration of mythological, allegorical and animal shapes, is executed in a Manneristic style of Italian derivation. The skillful, even "virtuoso" technique brings to mind the fact that in Nuremberg, at the end of the sixteenth century, the traditional test, which a goldsmith's apprentice had to pass in order to become a master of the guild, consisted of making three copies of a cup similar to this one. One of these is now in the Victoria & Albert Museum, London. The English term "masterpiece" derives from this feudal custom.

FLEMISH ART
Sacramental pyx
16th century.
Silver and *niello;*
diameter of the cover 4 3/8".

On page 138:
JOHN TURNER
Decorated jasper vase
18th century.
Ceramic with applied
reliefs of jasper;
height 11 7/8".

JOHN TURNER. *Decorated Jasper Vase.* *p. 138*
This vase was made according to the methods first developed by Josiah Wedgwood, the famous English designer and potter. Turner was one of his pupils. This technique, which makes use of different materials, consists of applying white stone to a blue ceramic base to achieve the impression of a cameo. This is a typical example of the Neo-Classic style, with its highly sophisticated, cool elegance.

GERMAN ART
Decorated silver cup
Nuremberg, 16th century.
Embossed and incised silver;
height 8".

ILLUMINATED MANUSCRIPTS

onginned godspell æft matheus

Incipit euangeli um secundum matthei
cuifter

ðæ
III III
lu III

uutedlice
ruæt pær
cnyster cneu
ne ro

rod lice

AUTE GENE

cynnætcenire t cneuueru ruæt ður pær mid h

RATIONIS GENERATIONUM
pær bi poeded t beboden t beræcrnud t betalit togenma
náller
banne

EXIIONBONIAA
moden hir abiach
dealdo
pær in
tid in
ralom
bircob
beod in
ioreph
gemen
robacob
anie
claeni

MATEREIUSMARICUOSEBI

EADFRITH OF LINDISFARNE. *Gospel Book.*

Presented in this chapter are some of the notable illuminated manuscripts from the collection of documents kept in the Department of Manuscripts of the British Museum. The collection consists of more than 150,000 pieces, with many works of great artistic and historical value.

Among the Celtic manuscripts, the *Lindisfarne Gospel* (ms. Cotton Nero D. IV) is outstanding. Both the text and the miniatures probably were executed by Bishop Eadfrith of Lindisfarne, which was one of the most important religious and cultural centers in Christianized Great Britain.

Illustrated here is a full-page reproduction of the X–P (*chi-rho*) leaf, from the beginning of the Gospel according to St. Matthew. The larger framework consists of horizontal and vertical lines, intersecting at right angles: this pattern is enclosed by the outlines of the decorations, the lines of script itself and the straight lines of the letters. It should be noted that the framework does not consist of uniform sections but is, instead, composed of lines repeated at varying intervals, forming a complex, articulated rhythm. The curving motifs of the capital letters — the X (*chi*) and P (*rho*) — relate to the rectilinear framework in swirling rhythms which are in a constant state of transformation. So all straight lines, which are limited to the letters and the frame, eventually become incorporated into the complex system of curving and spiral interlacings. These traceries, upon closer inspection, can be seen to consist of intertwined serpents, dragons and other fantastic animals, endlessly animating the length of the letters and the decorations. The whole complex is like a poem based on the varied repetition and linking together of the individual forms, in the rhythm of its lines, colors and forms that repeat themselves continuously, in an incessant oscillation from motif to motif. This reduces the myriad of rhythms to a single, very elaborate, yet figurative pattern. All this is, at the same time, a consistent reworking of ancient motifs, inherited from the Celts of East Europe and Central Asia, and adapted to rhythms partly derived from the Hellenistic Roman style with a new, disciplined sense of formal pattern and design.

GOSPEL BOOK. *St. Luke, England, Eighth Century.*

The decorations of this little *Gospel Book* (ms. Additional 40618) are a later product of the same artistic civilization as the Lindisfarne illuminations. Its history is unknown, but it can be ascribed to England at the beginning of the eighth century. The page with the figure of St. Luke is a typical example of a pattern regulated by strictly geometric principles. The proportions and size of the individual sections are fixed by the alternation of the squares and rectangles. The bases of the rectangles are equal to those of the squares: the height is equal to the length of the sides plus the diagonal. Such a decorative scheme, already in use, for example, in several pages of the *Lindisfarne Gospel* is found in Hellenistic Roman art. But in the Ireland and England it was developed with a new consistent, logical order. The decorative design was brought to its fullest development as the ultimate in the use of geometric patterns.

EADFRITH OF LINDISFARNE
X–P (chi-rho) Page
From the *Lindisfarne Gospel Book,*
Ms. Cotton Nero D. IV, sheet 29/r.
Lindisfarne, 698–721.
Miniature on parchment;
9 3/8″ × 8 1/8″.

ENGLISH MINIATURE
St. Luke the Evangelist
From the *Gospel Book*
Ms. Additional 40618, sheet 21/v.
England, early 8th century.
Miniature on parchment; 3″ × 4 1/8″.

CANTERBURY PSALTER. *David.*

The British Museum has an important example, dating from around the middle of the eighth century, of a special style of manuscript illustration which blends the stiff pattern of figure construction similar to that in use in the British Isles with a formal, Roman-derived style then in use in Continental Europe, above all in the Rhine district. The *Psalter of Canterbury* is so called because it comes from that abbey. Because of the complexity of its style, this work has been variously attributed to both the Rhineland and Canterbury, though the latter attribution is the one most frequently given. The page illustrated above, *King David and His Acolytes,* is executed according to a precisely measured plan: a square whose side is divided into five equal parts, or "modules"; these are in turn divided into five equal parts, or "sub-modules." The work also shows other influences, however. The construction of the arch is certainly similar to a late classic type, known indirectly through earlier English and Irish works. The stylized decoration of the arch and of the architectural framework repeats the motifs of the Celtic spirals and interlacings. The way the figure is posed is reminiscent of late classic, Constantinian sculpture, with its weighty forms and rhythmic patterns. These models of late Roman art are adapted to their new context in a provincial style which is found throughout Europe, even in areas close to the actual boundaries of the Roman Empire.

GOSPEL BOOK. *St. Matthew, Rhineland, ca. 800.*

Much more classical is this Gospel Book (ms. Harley 2788) made in the school of Charlemagne's court in the Rhineland, or somewhere in immediate contact with it, toward the end of the eighth century. The revival of Roman imperial culture which took place in his court at Aachen is re-

flected in all its arts, for instance in the Palatine Chapel of Aachen. This manuscript is one of the best examples of that school. The page reproduced here shows St. Matthew writing his Gospel. The composition reflects, it is true, complex mathematical relationships, but what predominates is a renewal of late Roman Imperial style, as well as that of the Byzantine art of Northern Italy. The canopy and building in the background, as well as the base of the throne, are reminiscent of buildings with a central, circular plan, like the Baptistery of the Lateran at Rome, or St. Vitale at Ravenna, as well as Carolingian architecture. A profound knowledge of the style of painting of the late Empire and the Exarchy is evident both in the depiction of the spacious backgrounds, which are almost three dimensional, and in the "impressionistic" technique. The artist, furthermore, knew the rules of perspective. This complex style in all probability drived from the then existing remains of Roman civilization in the region of Gaul and the Rhine, as well as from earlier illuminated manuscripts. It does not, however, constitute a completely isolated phenomenon, suddenly emerging at the Carolingian court, but occurs elsewhere, especially in central Europe.

BIBLE OF MONTIER–GRANDVAL. *Scenes with Moses.* *p. 143*
The author of the Bible of Montier-Grandval (ms. Additional 10546), from the abbey of that name near Tours, belonged to a culture that was not very different from the Carolingian Court. The page illustrated here, with *Moses Receiving the Tables of the Law* and *Moses Presenting Them to the People,* shows clearly the influence of the art of the 5th and 6th century: these are probably features derived indirectly from classicizing prototypes of the so-called "Carolingian Renaissance." This artist, however, gives new life and meaning to the culture he has inherited. Patterns here create perspectives as well as rhythms. The arches of the lower room correspond, for example, to those at the foot of the mountain, with the transition neatly marked by the beams of the ceiling. The figures are rendered in a clearly sculptural manner through a series of drapery folds that create a well ordered rhythm. This stylistic feature goes back to the formal, classical tradition of later Roman and Byzantine art, after the age of Constantine. Yet even these areas show the effect of the artist's rapid and allusive drawing, in a tradition of simplified, "impressionistic" lines and forms which first develops within ancient classical art and which can be seen even more clearly here, in the decoration above the columns and, above all, in the flame-shaped foliage of the trees in the background.

NEW TESTAMENT. *St. Luke, Constantinople, 10th Century.*
From among many Byzantine codices, we illustrate a typical product of the middle of the 10th century: the *Greek New Testament,* executed in Constantinople. On the page with the *Seated St. Luke,* we see once more the close dependence on forms of classical, Hellenistic and Roman art; here, however, Hellenistic features prevail in the musically rhythmic character of the work. The outer frame with its wavering, spiky decoration almost negates the straight lines that outline it, since the repetition reduces it to mere rhythm. Something very like this happens to the central scene: ulti-

MINIATURE FROM CONSTANTINOPLE
St. Luke the Evangelist
from the *Greek New Testament*
Ms. Additional 28815, sheet 76/v.
Constantinople, middle of 10th century.
Miniature on parchment; 5 1/8" × 6 3/4".

mately, by a complex system of inner proportions and correspondences, the composition is reduced to the inner arch, which stands symbolically for the inner space. Apparently sculptural or perspective elements, like the foreshortened throne and table, are only here as reflections of a prototype of this composition; a prototype which was certainly not a direct influence, but which was transformed through successive repetitions. The colors, distributed with thin, long strokes on the neutral gold and green background, also adds to the rhythm of the painting, rather than creating any real color contrasts. The result is a complete dematerialization of the image, which becomes an abstract presence in this extremely civilized, spiritualized, sophisticated work of art.

PSALTER. *The Annunciation, Rhenish, 11th Century.*

The use of rhythms, forms and styles of classical derivation continues in Continental Europe, particularly at the Ottonian court and in related circles; it can be seen, for example, in this *Psalter* which probably must be assigned to the Rhine region and to the beginning of the 11th century. In this work the continuity of classical Roman art through the Carolingian style is evident. The walled city in which the scene takes place is represented in a late classical manner: the earliest examples of such a schematic representation of city walls are to be found at Pompeii. The scheme is based on the proportions of the square. The central scene develops on either side of the diagonal of the square. The figures, which are sculptural, clear and distinct, are placed within an easily recognizable pattern. The movement of the square is stopped, so to speak, in the circle of the walls, and frames the scene itself in its width. The figures of the Angel and the Virgin, which are separated by the diagonal of the square, are also differentiated by the color contrast — red and pink on one side, green and blue on the other — ordered according to this same compositional pattern. The artist's classicism appears in his use of geometric principles of composition, as well as in the style of the figures, full of reminiscences of late antique and Carolingian forms.

PSALTER OF KING ATHELSTAN. *Christ in Majesty.*

Though the British Museum possesses an excellent collection of miniatures of other nations, the richest and most homogeneous series is that of English illuminations. The English miniatures added between 925 and 940 to the German *Psalter of King Athelstan* are one of the very first examples of Anglo-Saxon painting. The culture of those who carried out the work is very sophisticated and complex. In our illustration of *Christ in Majesty with Angels and Saints,* there are not many connections with preceding Irish and English styles; though we can compare the plant decorations of the frame to the similar decoration of the *Psalter of Canterbury.* The iconography of the single elements of the composition, the figures and forms, starting with the Christ in Majesty and the angels at the corners can be traced to Continental Europe, particularly Northern France. But the distribution and general disposition of the figures reveals itself as more unusual; even though, according to an almost constant Medieval rule, it is

ENGLISH MINIATURE
Christ in Majesty with Angels and Saints
from the *Psalter of King Athelstan*
Ms. Cotton Galba A. XVIII, sheet 21/v.
England, 925–940.
Miniature on parchment.

RHENISH MINIATURE
The Annunciation
Psalter illumination
Ms. Harley 2821, sheet 22/v.
Germany, beginning of 11th century.
Miniature on parchment.

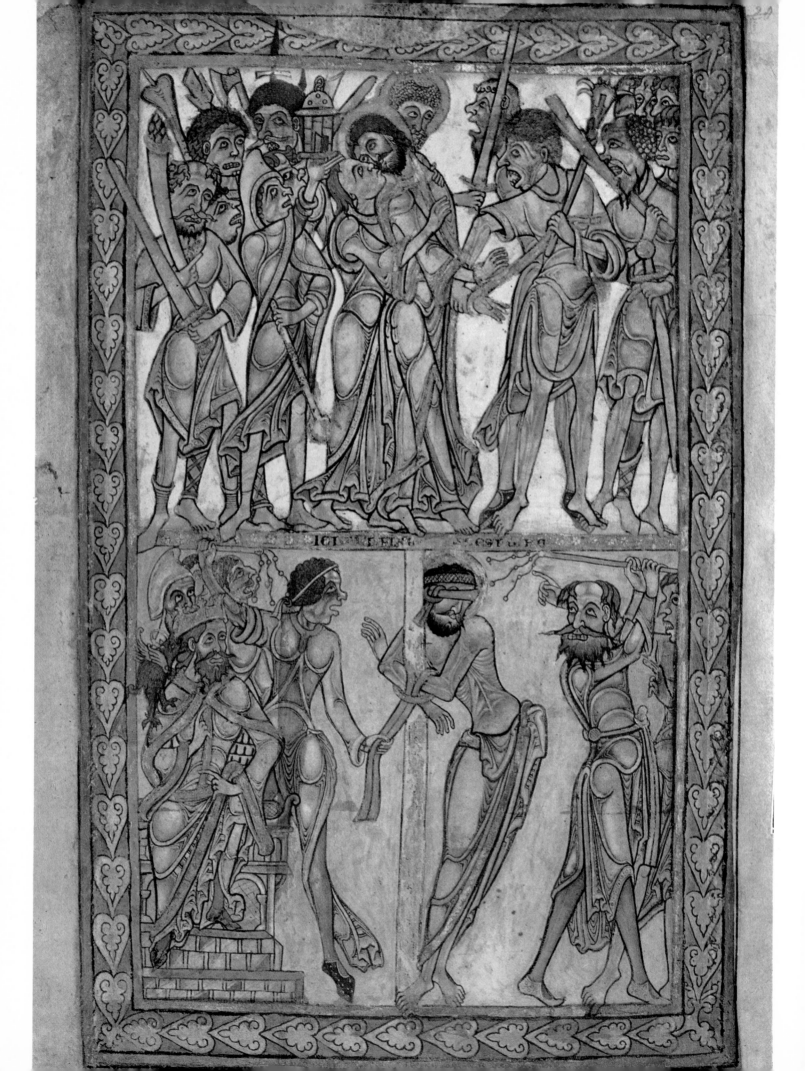

ICI · EST · LE · ·FLAGELE·

carried out in well-ordered "modular" patterns, in such a manner as to have the measure of each subsidiary element consist of a multiple or a submultiple of one of the main elements. A rare feature is the double almond (or mandorla) shaped frame, and the distribution of the space at the sides into three sections; within each layer, the saints are placed in superimposed rows, according to a scheme especially favored on late antique monuments of the Eastern Mediterranean, particularly in Syria.

PSALTER OF ST. SWITHUN. *Two Scenes from the Passion, Capture and Flagellation of Christ.*

In the manuscript known as the *Psalter of St. Swithun* or *of Winchester* or *of Henry of Blois,* which date from the middle of the twelfth century, the connection with the preceding products of that school of miniature painting is clear. In this page with the *Capture of Christ* and *The Flagellation,* the almost monochrome, graphic style accords with the Winchester tradition, but there are also strong connections with the art of more ancient times, as, for example, with Salzburg illuminations and Northern French miniatures.

In the harmonious rhythm of the whole, the artist has placed the figures in each group in the form of an elegant and elaborate arabesque. We can distinguish the clear partitions of pattern, starting with the diagonals which unite the two scenes into a single patterned rhythm. Such dematerialization of design belongs to an artistic tradition leading back, directly or indirectly, to the Hellenizing culture of Constantinople, at the time of the Commenes. The figures, within this rhythmic pattern, take on an almost musical meaning; even the faces of the executioners, ultimately derived from representations of the demons of ancient Greece and Rome, or from the bitter repertory of figures of contemporaneous Northern France, have their bestial features ordered in a beautiful cadence.

LIFE OF ST. CUTHBERT. *St. Cuthbert Sails over the Sea to Convert the Picts.*

The manuscript of the *Life of St. Cuthbert* by the Venerable Bede comes from the important religious and artistic center of Durham. Here again we are aware of a deep, well-assimilated culture. This artist is, indeed, clearly characterized as an individual. At the same time he makes use of the figurative style of 13th-century England, France and Germany, which we can identify from the presence of common features, particularly the colors. The illustrations of this manuscript, which are closer to German than to French models, attain, with the stark simplicity of the figures, a singularly inspired graphic, linear effect. This is clear in the composition reproduced below, showing St. Cuthbert on his way to convert the Picts. The strong diagonal waves in the lower part contrasts with the upper part where the curve of the boat is repeated by the foreshortened curve of the sail, with an almost perspectival viewpoint. In the context of such a perspective, perhaps, the stylization of the faces and of the drapery recover a sculptural value that had long been lost. Yet even this search for mass relates not to space, but to rhythm. In effect it seems to flatten the curve of the boat into a plane perpendicular to the spectator.

BEATUS FROM SAN DOMINGO DE SILOS. *Two Scenes of the Apocalypse.*

The *Commentary on the Apocalypse* by Beatus of Liebana from the monastery of San Domingo de Silos, to be dated 1091–1109, is one of the most remarkable examples of the so-called "Mozarabic" miniature. In this as in similar products, the figurative repertory relates to those in Carolingian codices, joined to elements derived from the whole Islamic world, from Syria to Spain. These two cultures both derived from Hellenist Rome, yet there is no doubt that at this point, when they meet, they produced a very strange, strong figurative style. In the pages illustrated here, the formation of patterns by the use of flat colors in the backgrounds is evident. This color pattern results in rhythmically ordered series of horizontal bands, often equal in size, which conform to the lines of script forming the basic pattern of the page. The rendering of drapery and shadows is derived from Syrian art, but, following the Hellenistic Roman tradition, they are presented as series of lines creating brief, independent rhythms. Color rhythms prevail in the extreme simplification of the contours of the figures, strong contrasts, or an affinity of colors and shades, result in lively distinctions and violent dissonances. The contours of the figures, which are extremely

SPANISH MINIATURE
The Four Horsemen of the Apocalypse
from the *Commentary on the Apocalypse*
by Beatus of Liebana
Ms. Additional 11695, sheet 102/v.
8″ × 12 1/2″.

SPANISH MINIATURE
*The Open Temple, the Eagle
and the Seven Angels with Phials*
from the *Commentary on the Apocalypse*
by Beatus of Liebana
Ms. Additional 11695, sheet 172/r.
S. Domingo de Silos, 1091–1109.
Miniature on parchment; 9 1/4″ × 13″.

simplified, connect with each other by means of hooked patterns which join them; yet in the end it is the alternation and contrast of the colors which dominate.

THE STATUTES OF WINCHESTER. *Scene of Offering.*

The *Statute of the New Minster of Winchester* is dated 966. The *Page of the Dedication* is framed in the usual rectangles whose height and width have a ratio equal to that of the diagonal and the side of a square. Both the frame and the figures clearly form an arabesque on the undecorated parchment background, just as in the style of late antiquity, for example at Ravenna, figures are represented against a neutral background. The most immediate precedent for this is the Metz school, from whence the artist of this manuscript drew inspiration for the nervous and fiery execution of the forms. These have very uneven contours; each is broken into complex little inner parts. Yet we still find an all-inclusive rhythm, starting with the pulsating quality of the foliage in the frame. The adapted forms of contemporaneous Rhenish classicism lose their sculptural consistency

151

to become a part of a design formed by nervous, rapid dashes. The image consists of a regular succession of arabesques; the colors play a minor role.

ENGLISH MINIATURE
The Visitation
from the *Psalter*
Ms. Cotton Caligula A. VII, sheet 4/v.
England, 12th century.
Miniature on parchment 5 3/8″ × 8 1/2″.

PSALTER.   *The Visitation, England, 12th Century.*
A highly developed, coherent style is shown in this *Psalter* of the 12th century.

In *The Visitation,* we see an original, conscious choice of some of the most important elements of medieval art. The strongly rhythmic frame composed of opposed triangles derives from Ottonian art, but the gilt background is decorated with flower-clusters developing according to typically Byzantine patterns and rhythms. Byzantine, too, are the elongated proportions of the figures, though the figures themselves recall French prototypes in coloring and in style. From so many easily detectable and varied influences, this artist has achieved a consistent style, chiefly by means of a calculated reduction of figurative elements to their bare essentials. The zigzag of the frame corresponds to the intersection of the two figures, but between frame and figures, the gilt background is interposed, a background which is not neutral, but animated all over with a repeated, rhythmic, engraved pattern of plant motifs. These marginal elements, almost in a minor key — the zigzag, the engraved motifs — constitute the very space, a formal repertory around the central figures; they move simultaneously upward, together and apart, an illusion reinforced by the alternation of the red and blue-green colors.

BIBLICAL PARAPHRASE OF ELFRIC.   *The Building of the Tower of Babel.*
The metrical *Paraphrase of the Pentateuch and of Joshua of Elfric* from Canterbury, ca. 1030–1040, takes us to a very different cultural atmosphere.

The page illustrated here clearly shows a close relationship with similar scenes in Spanish works, both in the representation of figures and in the use of strong color contrasts in superimposed bands. But there also seem to be close ties with Northern French art, for instance in the "modular" disposition of fan-shaped patterns of the drapery. The result is a complex work in which various rhythmic systems are presented at the same time in the figures: some coincide and some are diagonal in relation to the network formed by perpendicular lines parallel to the frame. The composition clearly develops upward, but there are meanders and returns which vary and animate it. The linear network pattern constantly changes angles, according to more or less emphasized curves which help to effect these transitions. Such a system is also followed in the colors; the rhythm of the contrasting blues and reds of the bricks is repeated in the larger pattern of the figures' blue and red clothes.

ENGLISH MINIATURE
The Building of the Tower of Babel
from *Elfric, Metrical Paraphrase
of the Pentateuch and of Joshua*
Ms. Cotton Claudius B. IV, sheet 19/r.
England 1030–40.
Miniature on parchment; 8″ × 11 1/4″.

Propterea babiloniam contigit uocari ciuitate. babel. ij. hebrei confusione uocant. de campo ū sennaar in regione babilonis meminit sibilla dicens. turris aū altitudo cui causa diuise st lingue. duo milia centum septuaginta. ... tenere dicitur passum. paulati altius angustior coartata erat. ut pond imminens scalas sustetaret.

Hanc turre nembroth gigas construxit. Qui p confusione lingua rū migrauit ide ad psas. eosq igne colere docuit.

gentes. 7 diuisio terrarū facta. phalec genuit reu. ... qui seruch. qui nachor. qui ... regma filiū cuthus duos. hauile. filios. saba. 7 didan. ioseph ... dicit. saba. 7 iuda. quoq ... hesuior. thabrenis. inde cognomen suū reliquit. qui aū subditi ... sennaar egressus e ...

MENORAH. *Two Biblical Scenes, England, 13th Century.*

It is possible to call attention to only a few outstanding examples of the abundant production of England in the Gothic period. Notable is this richly illustrated Menorah from the end of the thirteenth century. The Temptation of Adam and Eve and Noah and the Ark are inscribed within a circular shape and painted on a blue checkered background. They create — with their light, almost imperceptible rhythm — a kind of hidden unity in the composition, in vertical, horizontal and diagonal direction. The motifs are the usual ones in French, English and German illuminated manuscripts. With Adam and Eve, the composition is worked out in a radial symmetry formed by the intersection of diagonal, vertical and horizontal lines, which weave in and out of the circular form. There is a uniform, symbolically balanced pattern, in which the curving snake becomes the note of variation. More moving, however, is the composition of *Noah and the Ark,* with its striking contrast of blue sky, with its rhythmic straight lines and green water, all arranged in undulating cadences. The ark, asymmetrically placed, offers a further contrast, which is not in itself dramatic, but which contributes to the variation of the whole.

HEBREW ENGLISH MINIATURE
The Original Sin; Noah and the Ark
from a *Menorah*
Ms. Additional 11639 sheets 520/v and 521/v.
England, late 13th century.
Miniature on parchment.

FRENCH APOCALYPSE. *Scene of the Apocalypse, England, 14th Century.*
Also organized according to a strict compositional scheme is the *French Apocalypse,* the miniatures of which were painted in England at the be-

ENGLISH MINIATURE
The Angel Leads St. John to Heaven
from the *French Apocalypse*
Ms. Royal 19. B. XII, sheet 5/v.
England, early 14th century.
Miniature on parchment; 11 1/4″ × 8 1/4″.

ginning of the fourteenth century. Though the picture of *The Angel Leading St. John to Heaven* is covered with light tints, almost like watercolor, its quality is almost exclusively linear. In a rhythm based completely on irrational relationships, the square of the illustration is broken up vertically, horizontally and obliquely into various areas. A slow, ascending rhythm, along the ladder, creates the pivotal point of the composition. This culminates in the complex form of the joined, twisting, intertwined hands of St. John and of the Angel. Around this central element, the picture is organized in a series of squares, each one defined by means of color. The lines of the cloud, in contrast to rectilinear edges of surrounding squares, are formed by musical meanderings. Similar forms are used in the figures of the Angel and St. John, as well as in the vegetation in the area below. This juxtaposition of strict geometrical rhythms with undulating movement reveals the sophisticated style of the artist.

HEBREW ENGLISH MINIATURE
The Hebrews Collecting Chaff
to Make Bricks;
The Hebrews Constructing a Building for
Pharaoh;
Moses and Aaron
Change Their Staff into a Serpent;
Moses and Aaron Change Water into Blood
from the *Haggadah*
Ms. Additional 27210, sheet 11/v.
England, early 14th century.
Miniature on parchment.

HAGGADAH.   *Four Stories of Moses, England, 14th Century.*

We return to the English Hebrew context of the beginning of the fourteenth century with this *Haggadah*.

These *Four Stories of Moses* are like the other miniatures which offer an illustrated interpretation of the text. All show scenes from a cycle. Here, against a gold background, decorated in a subtle, oblique network, the scenes are laid out, four to a page. They are meant to be read from the upper right across, just as the Hebrew language is written from right to left. The scenes are connected by the repetition of figurative elements, for example, the red robes above, Moses, Aaron and the Pharaoh below.

Nor does this narrative emphasis hamper the pictorial treatment of the material. The artist still works on a level of high formal elaboration, interpreting in a personal manner the various elements of English, French and German Gothic style, accentuating the musical cadences that interest him, and making full use of the varied repetition of iconographic and formal elements.

157

ILLUMINATED BIBLE OF HOLKAM HALL. *The Creation of the Animals.*

The *Illuminated Bible in French,* as it is called, of *Holkam Hall,* developed out of a similar cultural climate, but it is a work of an artist of altogether different talent and interests.

In the *Creation of the Animals* we see that in the placement of the figurative elements, the artist has followed a certain pattern, whose rhythm corresponds approximately to the oblique network behind the figure of God the Father. This framework is not, however, the principal interest of the artist. He wants rather to collect examples and to represent the various elements — the human figure, animals, plants — in a form as universally comprehensible to the knowledgeable as philosophical concepts expressed in words. It is this "scientific" approach, actually, that dominates the forms: the lion or the peacock or the unicorn must rationally correspond. Each shape, which is generally the result of historical traditions, rather than a direct observation of nature, contains its own traditional, internal rhythm, which is fitted into the whole.

ENGLISH MINIATURE
God Creating the Animals
from the *Illuminated French Bible of Holkam Hall*
Ms. Additional 47682, sheet 2/v.
England, early 14th century.
Miniature on parchment; 8 1/4" × 11 1/4".

THE WORKS OF CHRISTINE DE PISAN. *Dedication Scene.*   *p. 160*

One illuminated manuscript has been selected from the beginning of the fifteenth century out of the many thousands of fifteenth-century examples in the British Museum.

On its Dedication page, the close connection between the illuminator who executed it with the Limbourg brothers and with the Burgundian court arts is clear.

The scene unfolds within a sharp, shortened perspective which indicates that a curved mirror must have been used to map its volumes. In this space, the objects seem to be pushed out toward the spectator, the connections that exist between them have to be reinforced with colors.

The scene is, in fact, dominated by the alternation of the blue and gold of the tapestries, and by the red of the bed and couch. In the midst of this chromatic rhythm are the figures of Queen Isabel, Christine de Pisan and the ladies-in-waiting, their hairdos and dress strongly geometricized according to the fashion of the time. All are ultimately reduced to lyrical accents. What began as a genre scene thus takes on rhythmical, curvilinear cadences, arranged according to very close planes which shorten the depth of the scene and bring out the peculiar emphasis on perspective.

On page 160:
MINIATURE IN THE STYLE
OF THE LIMBOURG BROTHERS
Christine de Pisan Offers Her Works to Isabel of Bavaria, Queen of France
from the *Works of Christine de Pisan*
Ms. Harley 4431, sheet 3/v.
France, early 15th century.
Miniature on parchment; 5 5/8" × 7".

Oment deu li puistaunt. En leyr feloit oisels nolaunt Artes diuerses
feriz portaunt. A ceus q̄ estoient auenaunz de tere fint cretie erbes z flu
res. De queus les mixtes fount lins cures. Bestes sure tere: en elbe peisson
Bien ne est saunhus noun. Car pur luy tut estet. Ciel z tere z caunit q̄ est.
Cum ple pensoit z le vousist. Beeu tot fu feet ceo dirt lescrit. Rien ne fut de
fa mein. Fors home z femme ceo sorez certein. Tutes choses il feseit fluriste
                                                  E tut ple feloit pur hō ne seruir.

Tres excellent de grant haultesse
Couronnee puissant princesse
Tresnoble royne de france
Le corps enclin vers vous madresse
En saluant par grant humblece
Pry dieu quil vous tiengne en souffrance
Long temps vive et apres souffrance
De la mort vous doint la richece
De paradis qui point ne cesse
Et au monde sans decevrance
Paix ioye et toute reconuvvance
De quanque affiert a leece
Haulte dame en qui font tous biens
Et ma tressouveraine ie viens
Devers vous comme vo creature

Pource livre cy que ie tiens
Vous presenter ou il na riens
En hystoire nen escripture
Qui naye en ma pensee pure
Pris ou stile que ie detiens
Du seul sentement que ietiens
Des dons de dieu et de nature
Quoy que mainte aultre creature
En ait plus en fait et maintiens
Et font ou volume compris
Plusieurs livres esquieulx iay pris
A parler en maintes manieres
Differens et pource lempris
Que on en devient plus appris
Dois de diverses matieres

HISTORY OF THE MUSEUM
AND ITS BUILDING

THE COLLECTIONS

DEPARTMENT OF EGYPTIAN ANTIQUITIES
DEPARTMENT OF PRINTED BOOKS AND MANUSCRIPTS
DEPARTMENT OF ORIENTAL PRINTED BOOKS AND MANUSCRIPTS
DEPARTMENT OF BRITISH AND MEDIEVAL ANTIQUITIES
DEPARTMENT OF WESTERN ASIATIC ANTIQUITIES
DEPARTMENT OF ORIENTAL ANTIQUITIES
DEPARTMENT OF GREEK AND ROMAN ANTIQUITIES
DEPARTMENT OF ETHNOGRAPHY
DEPARTMENT OF PRINTS AND DRAWINGS
DEPARTMENT OF COINS AND MEDALS

Department of Egyptian Antiquities.
Although Sir Hans Sloane himself had collected about
150 ancient Egyptian items, mostly small divine figures,
it was the capitulation of the French army in Egypt in
1801 that brought the first accession of large sculpture.
Napoleon had attached savants to his army to watch for
antiquities: among the 20 items his perspicacity had thus
saved — for the British — was the Rosetta Stone, the
decipherment of whose hieroglyphic inscription however,
had, to depend on the skill of another Frenchman,
François Champollion.

Again in the early nineteenth century, the British consul-
general in Egypt, Henry Salt, assembled a collection of
colossal sculpture that was bought by the Museum,
which, ever since, has continued to acquire choice items
from private collectors. At the end of the century, E. A.
Wallis Budge, later Keeper but then a departmental assistant, began a series of visits to Egypt that brought the
Museum important historical and literary material as
well as such masterpieces as the Stele of Tjetji.

Meanwhile, Sir Flinders Petrie (1853–1942) was enun-
ciating the principles of systematic excavation and com-
parative archeology that now form the basis of Egypto-
logical research, and under the aegis of the British "Egypt
Exploration Society" he and others not only excavated
such historical sites as Abydos and Amarna, but also
pushed the frontiers of knowledge far back into prehistory.

The British Museum now, thanks to the skill of generations of collectors and scholars, possesses an Egyptian
collection second only to that in Cairo in its coverage
of all aspects of ancient Egypt, from the Pharaohs on
the throne to the ploughman in the fields.

Department of Printed Books and Manuscripts.
As one of the world's great libraries, the British Museum
can claim a much earlier origin than it can as a museum
stricto sensu. It was established in 1753 to house, with
the other collections, the Cottonian Library. This library,
of some 950 volumes, had been originated by a wealthy
man of letters and public affairs of the early seventeenth
century, Sir Robert Cotton (1571–1631). Additions were
made by his son and grandson, and the latter arranged
that on his death, which occurred in 1702, the Library
should become public property.

The formation of the Cottonian Library must be viewed
against the background of the Renaissance. In the spirit
of that new age, wealthy citizens were collecting manuscripts and printed books, following the lead of the po-
tentates who were establishing or expanding great libraries, such as Pope Nicholas V in the Vatican, François I of France at Blois or the Medicis in Florence.

The incipient nationalism that manifested itself in England as well as in the other European lands fired Sir
Robert Cotton with enthusiasm for documents of all
kinds relating to the history of his country. In one particular respect Cotton was favored by circumstances aris-
ing out of the Protestant Reformation — the concomitant
of the Renaissance in Northern Europe. When King
Henry VIII repudiated the supremacy of the Pope in
1534, he also initiated the dissolution of the English

monasteries. Now, ever since the first monasteries had
been founded in the seventh century, their libraries had
been the chief repositories, not only of religious books,
but also of secular literature, and in particular of historical chronicles.

The monasteries once dissolved, the contents of their
libraries were in the main dispersed at random, but
soon certain scholars such as Matthew Parker, Arch-
bishop of Canterbury (1504–1575) — who preceded Cotton in the Readership of the first Society of Antiquaries
in London — began to collect important manuscripts
from the libraries. Parker's collection is now in Cambridge; Cotton's was to form, a century and a half later,
the nucleus of the British Museum Library. The Cottonian manuscripts include four of the six extant *Anglo-
Saxon Chronicles* and an eighth-century copy of the Ec-
clesiastical History by Bede — all important source material for the Anglo-Saxon period. They also embrace outstanding examples of Anglo-Saxon manuscript illumination, such as the Lindisfarne Gospels, the Psalter from
Canterbury and the unique Vespasian text of the epic
Beowulf. Among important charters in the Cottonian
Library are two exemplars of Magna Carta, the Great
Charter of 1215.

The birthright provided the British Museum by Sir Hans
Sloane (1660–1753) has already been indicated in the
preface. Here it may be stated that his collection included some 4,100 manuscripts and 40,000 printed books.
Sloane's catholicity of interest is reflected in the contents
of his library, but his medical profession is well to the
fore, as in thirteenth-century French manuscripts on
medicine and in letters and notes written by outstanding
physicians of the seventeenth and eighteenth centuries.
Oriental manuscripts also came Sloane's way, as for instance a version of Aristotle's *Historia Animalium* in
Hebrew written in the fifteenth century, and the hand-
somely illustrated *Pasaname.*

A third great library, apart from those of Cotton and
Sloane, was acquired by Parliament in 1753 upon the
foundation of the British Museum. This was the collection of 7,660 manuscripts, including fine specimens from
almost every country in Europe, assembled by the first
two Earls of Oxford, Robert and Edward Harley. The
Harleian Manuscripts are particularly concerned with the
history of the Bible and of the Christian church, with
English and French history and with Greek and Latin
classical literature, but they also contain many important
Turkish and Hebrew items.

Four years after its foundation, the British Museum received as a gift from King George II the collection known
as the "Old Royal Library." This consists of manuscripts
and printed books acquired by kings and queens of England from Edward IV (reign 1461–1483) onwards. Edward's Flemish taste, acquired through residence at
Bruges influenced subsequent work, for instance the manuscript of about 1500 of the poems by Charles Duke of
Orléans during his imprisonment in the Tower of London. King Henry VII added books printed on vellum —
in the pretentious fashion of the day — by the noted
Paris printer Antoine Vérard; Henry VIII acquired choice
specimens from the dissolved monasteries.

Scholarly works were obtained by the first Stuart king, James, especially from the library of the classical scholar Isaac Casaubon (1559–1614); the untimely death of James diverted to his successor Charles I an important gift intended for himself, the fifth century A.D. Greek biblical manuscript known as the *Codex Alexandrinus.*

From 1707 onwards, the Royal Library had been accommodated with the Cottonian. When they were incorporated in the British Museum, the depletion of the royal bookshelves was made good by King George III who inaugurated a library by buying a substantial collection of books assembled by Joseph Smith, British consul in Venice. The king's librarian had the benefit of the advice of the celebrated Samuel Johnson who stated in 1768: "A royal library should have at least the most curious edition, the most splendid and the most useful. The most curious edition is commonly the first, and the most useful may be expected among the last . . . The most splendid, the eye will discern." In 1823 King George IV transferred the King's Library, except for 30 of the choicest volumes, to the British Museum.

To accommodate the additional volumes, the 100-yard-long *salon* still called "The King's Library" was built in 1826 as an addition to the existing Museum building. King George III also inaugurated a "King's Music Library," particularly rich in autograph and printed music of Handel. Although this library has been accommodated in the Museum since 1911, it was not until 1957 that the Music Library became officially part of the Museum collections through the generosity of Queen Elizabeth II. The Harleian and Old Royal Libraries had also included musical items — the musical interests of Henry VIII being exemplified in the latter. Apart from the Royal gift the most important musical acquisition in recent times has been the purchase in 1946 of the Paul Hirsch Music Library, described as "one of the last great German private libraries of music," and particularly rich in early editions of Beethoven, Mozart, Schubert and Haydn.

The example of the Royal benefactors of the Museum Library has been repeatedly followed since the eighteenth century in the gifts and bequests of many devoted collectors, some among whom also provided funds to continue the collections. Space is not available to give details: such accessions range from incunabula to the correspondence of eminent statesmen of recent times.

At the outset, Sir Hans Sloane's collection had included 4,100 manuscripts; the "additional manuscripts," as they are officially called to distinguish them from Sloane's own, now number some 50,000. Together with about 75,000 "additional" charters and some 3,000 Greek and Latin papyri, they provide material for research in a wide variety of fields. Among printed books, the incunabula include Bibles and a Psalter printed on the press at Mainz with which the name of Gutenberg is connected, and also copies of the *Canterbury Tales* of Geoffrey Chaucer. Among the literary treasures of the seventeenth century, the "First Folio" of 1623, the first collected edition of the plays of William Shakespeare, is of outstanding interest; the works of the great philosopher Francis Bacon are also well represented appropriately enough, for Bacon was one of the regular users of the Cottonian Library before it became public property.

Direct purchase of books, by Parliament or by the Trustees of the Museum, or even by the sovereign, has always contributed to the growth of the Library. Thus, in 1762 King George III bought for the Museum a well-known collection of books, newspapers and pamphlets of the seventeenth century, which Thomas Carlyle described as "the most valuable set of documents concerned with English history." A similar collection bearing on the French Revolution was bought in 1831 and 1856, while one of the most important manuscript purchases of recent times was that of the Codex Sinaiticus, a great Bible of the fourth century A.D.

The steady growth of the Library was inevitable once the Old Royal Library came to the British Museum in 1757, for with it there came also the right to one copy of every work published in Great Britain and Ireland.

This provision is now embodied in the British law relating to copyright.

A beginning was made in the provision of special storage space for the Library with an iron bookstack running the whole length of the "King's Library." This was the forerunner of the "Iron Library" completed in 1857. This "Iron Library," and the Reading Room it surrounds, were conceived by Antonio (later Sir Anthony) Panizzi, Keeper of Printed Books 1837–56 and Principal Librarian (i.e. the chief officer of the Museum) 1856–66. Panizzi's scheme was worked out in detail by the architect Sydney Smirke, who succeeded his brother Sir Robert Smirke as architect to the British Museum.

Sir Robert's plan had provided a quadrangular building round a circular central space: when the increasing number of readers in the mid-nineteenth century impinged on the existing accommodation, it was an obvious solution to use the vacant central space. The domed reading room — with accommodation for some 400 readers — is surrounded by galleries for storage originally constructed in cast-iron, but now partly replaced by concrete structures. The design of central reading-room with surrounding bookstacks was later imitated in such buildings as the Library of Congress, Washington (1897) and the Prussian State Library, Berlin (1914).

The deviser of the Reading Room, Panizzi, had come to England in 1822 as a political refugee from Modena. His energy and organizing ability brought the Library, until then lagging behind those of other countries, into the forefront of world library practice. Panizzi's idealism may be discerned in words he wrote in 1836: "I want a poor student to have the same means of indulging his learned curiosity, of following his natural pursuits, of consulting the same authorities, as the richest man in the kingdom, as far as books go." Another glimpse of Panizzi's character is provided by the fact that — due probably to his innate Italian patriotism — he saw to it that the dome of the Reading Room was made slightly shorter in diameter than that of the Pantheon in Rome, the world's largest.

The present Reading Room and its predecessors have numbered many famous literary figures among their users, such as the historians Gibbon, Carlyle and Macaulay; the novelists Dickens and Thackeray; the statesman Disraeli and the dramatist G. B. Shaw: while from other countries such men as Louis Napoleon, Cavour, Garibaldi, Kossuth and Karl Marx have taken intellectual refuge in the British Museum Library in troubled times. It goes without saying that the contents of the library match in their variety the throng of readers that make use of them, and that such manuscript as that of *Alice's Adventures Underground* is preserved with as much care as the most solemn of state papers.

Though exact statistics are impossible, it was estimated that in 1965 there were between 6 and 7 million printed books in the British Museum, apart from the manuscripts and other items such as maps, music, postage-stamps and periodicals. For the accommodation of the books, nearly 90 miles of shelving are used, and the annual increment involves bringing into use each year 1 1/4 miles more. Newspapers, in about 400,000 volumes, are already accommodated in a separate building, opened in 1905 elsewhere in London. In the meantime, in order to provide for a fuller use of the Library's resources, plans have been drawn up for a completely new building on a site adjacent to that now occupied by the Museum.

Department of Oriental Printed Books and Manuscripts. Among the true adventurers, Sir Aurel Stein (1862–1943) cannot fail to receive mention in any account of cultural interchange between East and West. His travels in remote areas from Iran to Kan-su resulted, not only in archeological discoveries of high significance, but also provided the British Museum with over 6,000 manuscripts and printed rolls that had for centuries been walled up in a cave temple at Tun-huang in Sinkiang, among them the Diamond Sūtra, the oldest dated (868 A.D.) specimen of printing known.

163

Many of the Persian and Turkish illuminated manuscripts that are now among the most graceful treasures of the British Museum have been carefully preserved since they were originally made for such eminent rulers as Akbar and reflect the interest in *belles lettres* that they displayed. The Indian Rajput-style paintings portray charm and sensitivity with no less exquisite taste. The dedication that stems from religious piety appears in the superb artistry of copies of the Koran and of the Hebrew scriptures and ritual books, while the interpretation of Christian iconography in terms of local idiom lends great interest to such manuscripts as the Armenian New Testament or the Ethiopian biblical texts.

Department of British and Medieval Antiquities.
It is noteworthy that the British Museum was over 100 years old when, in 1866, the name "British" was first used in a departmental title, that of the Department of British and Medieval Antiquities. After the enthusiasm for the classical world of Greece and Rome had run its course for two centuries, it was time for the homeland to receive attention. Documentary material for the historical past of Britain had, of course, been abundantly available from the start of the Museum, but, with scientific archeology yet in its cradle, there was a tendency to assume all prehistoric artifacts to be of one age — that of the "Ancient Britons" — just as in France it would be assigned to the Gauls or in Scandinavia to the Goths.

But Christian Thomsen in Denmark, Boucher de Perthes and Édouard Lartet in France, and William Pengelly and Henry Christy in Britain were making discoveries in the mid-nineteenth century that demonstrated that human beings must have existed much longer ago than the year 4004 B.C. of orthodox Biblical chronology. With the publication of Charles Darwin's *On the Origin of Species* in 1859 and of Sir Charles Lyell's *The Antiquity of Man* in 1863, the barriers to the understanding of man's past were at last demolished.

Accordingly, Sir Hans Sloane's description of a flint hand-axe in his collection as "a British weapon found with an elephant's tooth" seems ludicrous today, though his words aptly expressed the thinking of the eighteenth century. In the field of medieval antiquities, Sloane was of course on much surer ground, and could appreciate the merits of the jeweled sixteenth-century goblets he had procured.

The Department here under consideration is the most varied in scope, ranging from Stone Age artifacts to the European and Japanese timepieces comprised in what is acknowledged to be the world's finest horological collection. The care of so mixed a domain has demanded an unusual versatility in its Keepers, here a notable succession of scholars was headed in 1866 by Sir Wollaston Franks, who was instrumental in securing, not only the Treasure of the Oxus, but also the Royal Gold Cup of the Kings of France and England and the "Franks" Casket, an outstanding example of 8th-century craftsmanship from Northern England. Franks also initiated — and himself bequeathed much of — the Museum's ceramic collection in which the products of all important English and Continental factories are well represented.

The great amount of modern archeological activity is reflected in such finds as that of the Sutton Hoo Ship Burial, revealed in 1939 as England's richest archeological discovery to date, and in the fourth-century Romano-British mosaic floor found in southwest England in 1963, one panel of which is confidently interpreted as a portrait of Christ — a rarity for the period in Britain.

Department of Western Asiatic Antiquities.
The ancient civilizations of Western Asia remained virtually unknown for nearly a century after the foundation of the British Museum. In 1825, indeed, some fragments of sculpture from Persepolis reached London, and a small group of objects collected by Claudius James Rich on the sites of Babylon and Nineveh were purchased by the Museum, but it was not until sixteen years later that Austen Henry Layard (later Sir Henry) began to emulate the excavations of the Frenchman Paul-Emile Botta at Khorsabad in his own sensational discoveries at Nimrūd, Nineveh and Asshur.

Meanwhile, from Nineveh, over 20,000 cuneiform tablets came to London, where Henry Creswicke Rawlinson (later Sir Henry) was astounding the learned world by his exposition of their script. The texts and the inscriptions on the sculptures opened up a new vista of the life, history and thought of the ancient peoples of western Asia. The later excavations of Sir Leonard Woolley and others at Ur and the nearby site of Al-Ubaid added knowledge of the rich Sumerian culture to what was already known of Babylon and Assyria.

Between 1937 and 1949, Sir Leonard Woolley excavated at Atshanah (ancient Alalakh) near Antioch. Here, architecture, art and religious symbols demonstrated cultural connections from India to Crete.

Meanwhile, not only in southwest of Asia, but also in Iran, archeologists have abundantly shown how the whole region was a great cradle of civilization. Apart from scientific investigations, even chance finds like that of the "Treasure of the Oxus" have provided important evidence of the technical skill and living standards of the past.

Department of Oriental Antiquities.
One of the most devoted of the Museum's officers, Sir Augustus Wollaston Franks (1826–97) provided the Oxus Treasure as a bequest. Franks devoted his own resources of time and money to building up the Museum collections in fields ranging over practically the whole world: to Asia, he paid particular attention, assembling Turkish faïence, Islamic metalwork, Mughal jades, Chinese cloisonné, Arita enamels from Japan, among other treasures.

Arita ware also formed part of Sir Hans Sloane's collection, part of which he obtained from the Swiss collector Engelbert Kaempfer, who spent two years (1690–92) on Deshima Island as an embassy physician; it was at this time that Kaempfer acquired art objects, books and prints, including important early examples of seventeenth-century Chinese color-printing.

The many superb exhibits of Oriental art in the Museum stand as eloquent witness of the taste and generosity of generations of private collectors with the welfare of the national collections at heart; and many soldiers, scientists and administrators — particularly in the eighteenth and nineteenth centuries — developed appreciation of the cultures of distant lands and passed on their appreciation to fellow Westerners. If today nearly every country prevents the passage beyond its frontiers of evidence important for its artistic development, and the Western connoisseur must look to the sale-room rather than a tour of duty in the Orient to build up his collection, present realities should not obscure the devotion of such men as Colin Mackenzie who in 1797 discovered in the Deccan the stūpa of Amarāvatī or Sir Stamford Raffles (1781–1826) who while in Java assembled what is now the finest collection of Javanese sculpture outside Holland and Java itself.

Department of Greek and Roman Antiquities.
The origin of the Greek and Roman collections of the British Museum can be traced to the visits paid to the Mediterranean lands, under the influence of the Renaissance, by wealthy English collectors of the seventeenth and eighteenth centuries. Thomas Howard, Earl of Arundel (1585–1646) paid a prolonged visit to Italy in 1613 and conducted excavations in Rome. To him, it was said in a London publication of 1634, "this angle of the world oweth the first sight of Greeke and Romane Statues." The Arundel Collection was unfortunately dispersed in the late seventeenth century, but Sir Hans Sloane acquired some small items from it.

In the eighteenth century, when the Continental "Grand Tour" became part of the elegant Englishman's education, interest in the Mediterranean lands was further stimulated, and in 1734 a Society of Dilettanti — men devoted to the pursuit of antique art — was established in London; this Society was later to promote a number of excavations in Greece, from which items came to the British Museum.

The first important addition to the few classical antiquities of Sir Hans Sloane was made in 1772 when the British Parliament purchased the collection of Sir William Hamilton, Ambassador in Naples (1730–1803). This was followed in 1805 by the purchase of the collection of Charles Townley, a matrilineal descendant of the Earl of Arundel, who lived in Italy from 1708 to 1772 and had acquired — from Italian and English collectors, and from excavations of the time in Rome — sculpture with which to equip the "Roman Villa" in London to which he was willing to admit "men of taste" — the first hint of a museum that might be open to the public.

The outstanding acquisition of Greek sculpture was, however, the purchase in 1816 for £35,000 of sculptures from the Parthenon and Erechtheion in Athens — a collection which also included fragments from Mycenae, and which was known from the name of its owner as "The Elgin Marbles."

The Earl of Elgin had been appointed Ambassador to the Sublime Porte in Constantinople in 1799. Like other diplomats of the age, Lord Elgin sought to serve art as well as politics. He engaged a team of architects, draftsmen and cast-makers to record antiquities in Greece. But when he became aware of the neglect that the sculptures in Athens were suffering, the ambassador obtained official sanction to remove some works to "a place of greater safety." By the purchase of these sculptures after their arrival in England, Parliament assured them the security of the British Museum, where in 1962 most of them were accommodated in the latest addition to the museum buildings, the gallery that bears the name of its donor, Lord Duveen.

It is impossible to record here all the subsequent gifts, bequests and purchases of Greek and Roman antiquities, but mention must be made of the important series of excavations sponsored by the Museum itself in the mid-nineteenth century which resulted in the acquisition of outstanding sculpture from Asia Minor, including the sixth-century B.C. seated figures from Didyma and fourth-century and sixth-century sculptures from Ephesus and the fourth-century sculptures from the Mausoleum at Halicarnassos and from Cnidos.

By similar varied means comprehensive collections of Greek bronzes, terra cottas and vases reached the British Museum. The Roman material tends to attract less popular regard than the Greek, but mention may be made of the famous Portland Vase.

Department of Ethnography.
Sir Hans Sloane's collection included many items that he called "artificial curiosities." We should now describe them as "ethnographical specimens." His collection was formed early enough for it to contain important evidence for the life of primitive communities when they were still free of European colonial influence. As early as 1770, the Museum had benefited much from the Pacific voyages of such explorers as Captain James Cook (1728–79) who took a particularly lively interest in the various cultures he encountered. But it was not until Henry Christy (1810–65) established sound basic principles that ethnography was established as a scientific discipline. Christy had sought to correlate the study of European prehistory with that of extant primitive peoples, and when at his death he bequeathed his fortune and extensive collections to four trustees, one of them Sir Wollaston Franks, the trustees made over the collections to the British Museum, with funds to provide for future acquisitions. One of Christy's particular interests had been the early culture of the Americas, but by the turn of the century Africa, hitherto the "dark continent," had come into the political arena, and revealed itself to astonished Europeans as the seat, particularly in its western bulge, of cultures of a level as yet barely suspected.

Department of Prints and Drawings.
The Museum no longer maintains a collection of oil paintings, nevertheless, the Print Room contains one of the great European collections of prints and drawings, in which all European schools covering five centuries are abundantly represented. Medieval painting is, of course, mainly to be found in manuscript material, but the Museum's series of woodcuts, engravings and etchings runs parallel to its drawings from the fifteenth century to the present.

Thanks to Sir Hans Sloane, the Museum possesses what has become the second largest collections of drawings by Albrecht Durer in existence. The "International Gothic" style of the fifteenth century is represented by Bosch at one extreme and by the great Italian masters — Fra Angelico, Filippo Lippi and Pisanello — at the other. Mantegna, Verrocchio, Carpaccio and Antonio Pollaiuolo demonstrate the growing magnificence of the High Renaissance, in which Raphael and Leonardo da Vinci were dominant figures. Of Michelangelo, the Museum possesses one of his most important series of drawings.

Holbein's realistic portraiture can be related to the acute observation of Rembrandt, though the latter's originality sets him quite apart. Rembrandt's French contemporary Claude has an unrivaled representation in the British Museum. Goya presents realism in a new light in his incisive studies of humanity's inhumanity.

The drawings of the English school are naturally the best represented in the collection. The sixteenth-century portraitist and miniaturist Nicholas Hilliard is the earliest British artist of note of whom much detail is known — he was official "Limner" to Queen Elizabeth I. Turning to a later period, the incipient romanticism of Blake lay along the same path that brought Turner to create his atmospheric style — this artist's bequest in 1851 enriched the Museum with some 20,000 of his watercolours.

Apart from this unique bequest, most of the prints and drawings in the British Museum have been acquired either through the generous gifts or bequests of individuals, or through the operation of the National Art Collections Fund, which provides the means whereby all those who have the welfare of the nation's museums and art galleries at heart have an opportunity of making their financial contribution, large or small, towards increasing the range of the treasures that go to constitute the cultural heritage of the people — both of Britain and of the world.

The Department of Coins and Medals is based on the magnificent collections which had already been acquired by the Museum in the eighteenth century. The section on Greek arts was enriched by the Royal Collection, given to the Museum by George IV; to the section on Roman art were added, in the nineteenth century, the two important collections of the Count John F. W. de Salis, and of the Duke of Blacas. There is, besides, an enormous collection of Celtic and English coins, as well as one of Oriental coins, from the beautiful collection given by William Marsden to the Museum in 1834.

Frederick Sebastian Leigh-Browne

The Museum's splendid library of books, manuscripts, periodicals and newspapers, including a photograph and photocopy service, is open to the public. Special exhibitions of objects chosen from the various departments, are held periodically: there are also monthly lectures and daily guided tours. The Museum maintains its own research laboratory as a special department to take care of necessary restorations and give technical information about the objects in the collections. Finally, there are the Museum publications, which include the periodical *The British Museum Quarterly*, with its reports of new acquisitions and scholarly articles on objects from the collections, as well as numerous monographs on the various sections of the departments, catalogues of the various departments and a number of guidebooks.

THE BUILDING

Since the British Museum could not be adequately housed in any building already in existence — as was the case for so many other European museums which grew within older palaces and noble houses — a new building was designed especially for it and erected at the beginning of the nineteenth century. This building grew along with the collections it housed. In 1846 the gallery built for the Townley Collection was torn down: the oldest part of the present building is therefore the great Library, called the King's Library, built between 1823 and 1828 by Sir Robert Smirke for the enormous collection of books given by George IV to the Museum.

It was clear even then that the whole Museum needed a larger complex in which to expand. In 1827 construction began on two wings of the future four-sided building, again following Smirke's plans. In 1846 the old Montagu House was torn down to make room for the present building, under the direction of the brother of Smirke. The building, finished in 1852, is in that Neo-Classic style which fitted so well with the archeological taste of the period, The Greek Revival; another great museum, the Altes Museum in Berlin, designed by Schinkel, was also conceived in that style. The colonnaded façade, its pediment filled with a statue group representing the "Progress of Civiliza-

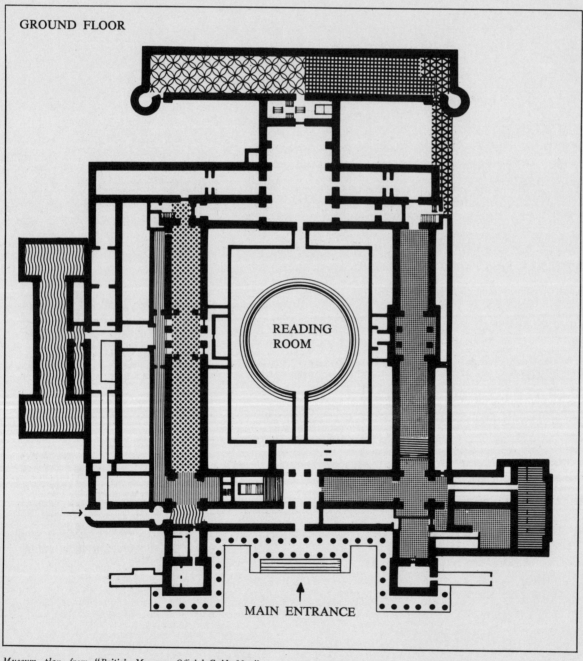

GROUND FLOOR

READING ROOM

MAIN ENTRANCE

166

Museum plan from "British Museum Official Guide Map"

tion," by Westmacott, was evidently intended to suggest a "temple of art," with the optimistic belief in progress typical of the age.

The newly constructed sections were still not large enough, however. In 1857 the central courtyard had already been taken over as a new reading room and storerooms for the library. These were built according to the plans of Anthony Panizzi, the Italian patriot who became, during his exile in England, Librarian of the British Museum (1856–66). In 1888 it became necessary to house the Natural History collections separately, in South Kensington; at the same time a gallery was built especially for the marbles from the Mausoleum of Halicarnassus which had been sent to England by the Sultan Abdul Medjid; and a wing was constructed for the collection of manuscripts, prints and drawings.

In this century further construction was made possible especially by two donors. In 1914 the King Edward Building was completed with funds from a gift made in 1900 by Vincent Stuckey Lean as well as funds allocated by Parliament for this purpose. The new gallery to the north of the preceding building houses objects from The Departments of Oriental Antiquities, British and Medieval Antiquities, and Coins and Medals. The gallery to the west, built by 1938 to exhibit the sculptures from the Parthenon, is due to the generosity of Lord Duveen. At the present moment a general plan is under way to modernize and enlarge the whole arrangement of the galleries.

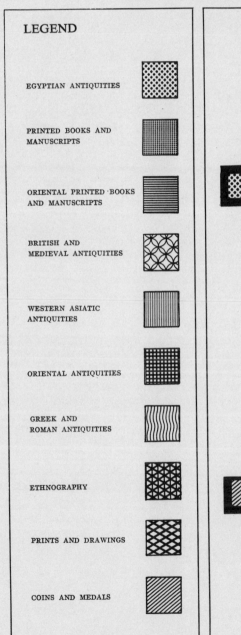

LEGEND

EGYPTIAN ANTIQUITIES

PRINTED BOOKS AND MANUSCRIPTS

ORIENTAL PRINTED BOOKS AND MANUSCRIPTS

BRITISH AND MEDIEVAL ANTIQUITIES

WESTERN ASIATIC ANTIQUITIES

ORIENTAL ANTIQUITIES

GREEK AND ROMAN ANTIQUITIES

ETHNOGRAPHY

PRINTS AND DRAWINGS

COINS AND MEDALS

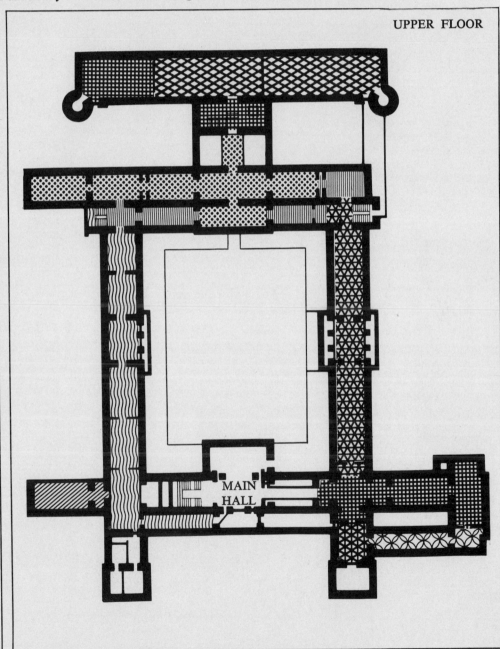

UPPER FLOOR

MAIN HALL

BASIC BIBLIOGRAPHY

EARLY GUIDEBOOKS: *There exist a few old guidebooks which contain useful information on the history of the Museum and its collections. Of particular value are the following:*

A Synopsis of the Contents of the British Museum, LONDON, G. WOODFALL & SON, 1851.

EDWARD A. BOND, A Guide to the Exhibition Galleries of the British Museum, LONDON, WOODFALL & KINDER, 1879.

MONOGRAPHS: EDWARD EDWARDS, Lives of the Founders of the British Museum, LONDON, 1870.

ARUNDELL ESDAILE, The British Museum Library, LONDON, 1940.

CATALOGUES: *There is a complete inventory of all the catalogues of the departments, available at no cost upon request:*
List of Catalogues, Guide Books and Facsimiles.

MODERN GUIDEBOOKS: The British Museum, A Guide to its Public Services, THE TRUSTEES OF THE BRITISH MUSEUM, LONDON, 1962.

Guide and Map to the British Museum, THE TRUSTEES OF THE BRITISH MUSEUM, LONDON, 1967.

We are grateful to the following for their kind assistance:
M. R. Taylor and E. F. Chapman-Purchas of the Department of Medieval Antiquities, and E. H. Cuthbert of the Department of Greek and Roman Antiquities of The British Museum, and to Prof. Gian Lorenzo Mellini, art historian at the University of Pisa.

INDEX OF ILLUSTRATIONS

INDEX OF NAMES

GENERAL INDEX